REAPING THE BENEFITS OF INDUSTRY 4.0 THROUGH SKILLS DEVELOPMENT IN HIGH-GROWTH INDUSTRIES IN SOUTHEAST ASIA

INSIGHTS FROM CAMBODIA, INDONESIA, THE PHILIPPINES, AND VIET NAM

JANUARY 2021

ASIAN DEVELOPMENT BANK

 Creative Commons Attribution 3.0 IGO license (CC BY 3.0 IGO)

© 2021 Asian Development Bank
6 ADB Avenue, Mandaluyong City, 1550 Metro Manila, Philippines
Tel +63 2 8632 4444; Fax +63 2 8636 2444
www.adb.org

Some rights reserved. Published in 2021.

ISBN 978-92-9262-466-8 (print); 978-92-9262-467-5 (electronic); 978-92-9262-468-2 (ebook)
Publication Stock No. SPR200328
DOI: http://dx.doi.org/10.22617/SPR200328

The views expressed in this publication are those of the authors and do not necessarily reflect the views and policies of the Asian Development Bank (ADB) or its Board of Governors or the governments they represent.

ADB does not guarantee the accuracy of the data included in this publication and accepts no responsibility for any consequence of their use. The mention of specific companies or products of manufacturers does not imply that they are endorsed or recommended by ADB in preference to others of a similar nature that are not mentioned.

By making any designation of or reference to a particular territory or geographic area, or by using the term "country" in this document, ADB does not intend to make any judgments as to the legal or other status of any territory or area.

This work is available under the Creative Commons Attribution 3.0 IGO license (CC BY 3.0 IGO) https://creativecommons.org/licenses/by/3.0/igo/. By using the content of this publication, you agree to be bound by the terms of this license. For attribution, translations, adaptations, and permissions, please read the provisions and terms of use at https://www.adb.org/terms-use#openaccess.

This CC license does not apply to non-ADB copyright materials in this publication. If the material is attributed to another source, please contact the copyright owner or publisher of that source for permission to reproduce it. ADB cannot be held liable for any claims that arise as a result of your use of the material.

Please contact pubsmarketing@adb.org if you have questions or comments with respect to content, or if you wish to obtain copyright permission for your intended use that does not fall within these terms, or for permission to use the ADB logo.

Corrigenda to ADB publications may be found at http://www.adb.org/publications/corrigenda.

Notes:
In this publication, "$" refers to United States dollars.
ADB recognizes "China" as the People's Republic of China and "Vietnam" as Viet Nam.

Cover design by Mike Cortes.

Contents

Table, Figures, and Boxes	iv
Foreword	vi
Preface and Acknowledgments	viii
Abbreviations	x
Executive Summary	xi
Chapter 1: The Industry 4.0 Skills Challenge	**1**
Industry 4.0 and Its Relevance for Cambodia, Indonesia, the Philippines, and Viet Nam	1
Industry Selection	3
Relevance of Industry 4.0	7
Skills Demand Analysis	9
Skills Supply Trends	15
Chapter 2: Overview of the Training Landscape	**18**
Industry 4.0 Readiness	18
Curricula	19
Industry Engagement	21
Teachers, Trainers, and Instructors	24
Performance and Policy Support	24
Supply and Demand Mismatches	26
Chapter 3: National Policy Responses	**28**
Review of Industry 4.0 Policy Actions in Each of the Four Countries	28
Assessment of Implementation Approach	35
Chapter 4: The Way Forward	**41**
The COVID-19 Effect	41
Facing the Four Countries	42
Recommendations to Address Challenges	43
Bibliography	**52**

Table, Figures, and Boxes

Table
Examples of 4IR Skills-Related Best Practices from Around the World   43

Figures
1	What is Industry 4.0?	2
2	Variation in Companies' Understanding of 4IR	7
3	Sentiment toward the Adoption of 4IR Technologies	8
4	Expected Productivity Improvement from 4IR Technologies in 5 Years	8
5	Modeled Impact of 4IR on Job Number Change from 2018 to 2030	9
6	Job Displacement Effect of 4IR Technologies modeled for 2030	12
7	How Employers Expect 4IR to Affect Time Spent on Tasks by Type from 2018 to 2025	13
8	Relative Importance of Occupational Skills in 2030	16
9	Additional Training Required by 2030 by Industry and Training Channel	16
10	Training Institution Perceptions of Their Readiness for 4IR	19
11	How Frequently Institutions Review and Update Curricula	20
12	Share of Learning Time by Type of Training	21
13	Prevalence of Technology Courses and Technology-Assisted Delivery in Training Institutions	22
14	Programs Provided in Addition to Training Courses	23
15	Frequency of Training Institution Communication with Employers	23
16	Training Institutions' Partnerships and Engagement with Industry	24
17	Institutional Support for Instructors and Teaching Staff	25
18	Difficulty of Filling Student Spots in Training Institutes	25
19	Policies that Institutions Say Could Help Them the Most	26
20	Reasons Students Cannot Find Jobs after Graduation, by Prevalence	27
21	Perceptions of How Well Graduates Are Prepared for Entry-Level Positions	27
22	Strength of Focus on 4IR Policy Action, by Country	29
23	The Implementation of Education, Jobs, and Skills Policy Responses to 4IR, by Country	37
24	Recap of 4IR Challenges	42

Boxes

1	Estimating Employment Changes	10
2	Equity Concerns Related to Industry 4.0	11
3	Estimating Task Shifts	14
4	Estimating Skills Changes	15
5	Estimating Training Requirements	17
6	Singapore's Industry Transformation Maps	44
7	Connecting Students and Industry with Boot Camps	45
8	Leveraging Technologies to Improve Education and Address Gender Inequality	46
9	The Malaysian Skills Certification Program	47
10	Incentive Schemes in the Region for Training by Firms	49

Foreword

Talent and skills are valuable in powering knowledge-based economies. The Fourth Industrial Revolution (4IR) has ushered in extraordinary technological advances, fusing boundaries of physical, digital, and biological worlds to create new paradigms in the way we live, work, and interact. These trends have heralded excitement and fear—excitement in advancing frontiers of human endeavor and fear of negative repercussions on jobs and rising inequalities.

To respond to questions and concerns in developing member countries of the Asian Development Bank (ADB) on how their economies can transition effectively to 4IR, the study *"Reaping the Benefits of Industry 4.0 Through Skills Development in High-Growth Industries in Southeast Asia"* builds an evidence based on opportunities, challenges, and promising approaches in 4IR. It covers Cambodia, Indonesia, the Philippines, and Viet Nam with specific focus on two industries in each country deemed important for growth, employment, and 4IR: tourism and garments in Cambodia, food and beverage manufacturing and automotive manufacturing in Indonesia, information technology and business process outsourcing and electronics in the Philippines, and agro-processing and logistics in Viet Nam.

Much has been written about anticipated loss of millions of jobs arising from automation. At ADB, we take a tempered view. The study reaffirms a positive outlook to 4IR creating new opportunities for quality jobs. While many jobs will indeed be lost as a result of automation, new jobs will emerge through the adoption of technologies that will increase worker productivity and competitiveness of nations, thereby leading to greater prosperity. However, tapping such benefits is predicated on increasing investments in skills development and greater efforts by companies to upskill their workforce to perform new and higher order roles in complementarity with machines.

Adoption of 4IR technologies can increase efficiency and productivity. They enable real-time tracking of supply chains for production and inventory management of raw materials and finished goods. Use of artificial intelligence and machine learning can provide insights into consumer behavior to customize production. Robotic process automation can relieve tedious and repetitive labor-intensive activities, allowing time for higher order functions. Augmented reality and virtual reality can be helpful to train workers in new tasks that they were not familiar with, or skilled in, earlier. Application of 4IR technologies helps developing countries move up the value chain in their products and services. Timely skills development can ensure that automation and artificial intelligence can benefit workers at large.

The study has resulted in a suite of country reports for Cambodia, Indonesia, the Philippines, and Viet Nam, and a synthesis report that captures common elements across the four. They seek to provide policy makers with research and evidence-based solutions for skills and talent development to strengthen the countries' readiness for a transition to 4IR.

The role of governments is crucial in ensuring equitable access to skills development. We expect to see a new balance between physical and virtual workplaces as the gig economy, where employers increasingly rely on part-time freelance workers on short-term contracts, takes firmer position, and widespread digital transformation of citizen services that call for basic digital capabilities in all population groups and rising opportunities for those with advanced digital skills. Job losses will be real, however, a well-prepared 4IR strategy with industry transformation road maps that are recommended in the study can convert disruptions to opportunities to pivot the workforce to new and modern occupations.

The study was completed prior to the coronavirus disease (COVID-19). It is apparent that COVID-19 is accelerating digital transformation. Companies deploying 4IR technologies are likely to recover faster from heavy disruptions arising from the pandemic and be more resilient in the future. Beyond COVID-19, market analysts predict a 'new normal' where digital strategies adopted during the lockdown due to the pandemic will pick up pace. Consumer and producer behavior will most likely be altered permanently with greater digital exposure. The study's recommendations to strengthen widespread digital capabilities, enhance online/distance learning, digital platforms, education technology (EdTech), and simulation-based learning have become more relevant in the aftermath of COVID-19. The study also points to the scope for closer collaboration between public and private sectors, which is also quite relevant in the COVID-19 context. The findings of this study are thus very timely in the discourse to facilitate a sustainable recovery from COVID-19, as countries aspire for accelerating economic diversification and boosting competitiveness using the pandemic as an opportunity for structural reforms.

We welcome your feedback on this report and continued engagement with all stakeholders.

Woochong Um
Director General
Sustainable Development and
Climate Change Department

Ramesh Subramaniam
Director General
South East Asia Department

Preface and Acknowledgments

The ADB study *Reaping the Benefits of Industry 4.0 Through Skills Development in High-Growth Industries in Southeast Asia* marks our effort to bridge research, policy, and practice on the implications of the Fourth Industrial Revolution (4IR) on future job markets. To effectively address this forward-looking topic, the study made use of various sources of secondary information and sought to triangulate information from different primary sources. It included a survey of employers, a survey of training institutions on their readiness for 4IR, and analysis of data from online job portals from each country to assess trends in skills demand. The study used a modeling exercise to estimate job displacement and gains in the selected industries in each of the countries. A review of the policy landscape based on benchmarks from international trends and experiences provides the basis for the action points that countries can use to harness the potential of Industry 4.0 to increase productivity, facilitate skills development, and incentivize industry.

The findings and recommendations from the study point us to collaborate with our partners to implement decisive changes in renewing skills development strategies that acquire a full life cycle approach to skills development. This means that there are no degrees or certificates for life and constant renewals and upskilling are essential. The preponderant focus on institution-based training needs to give way to more flexible and multimodal training to include bootcamps, e-learning, and work-place based training. Training for digital skills at basic, intermediate, and higher levels needs a significant ramp up as workplaces undergo digital transformation.

As co-team leaders, we thank the consultant team led by Fraser Thompson, director, AlphaBeta, for an excellent partnership in this study. The core team in AlphaBeta include Konstantin Matthies, engagement manager; Genevieve Lim, engagement manager; and Richard McClellan, senior advisor. We thank AlphaBeta's national experts Ananto Kusuma Seta (Indonesia), Dao Quang Vinh (Viet Nam), Jose Roland A. Moya (Philippines), and Trevor Sworn (Cambodia). AlphaBeta's team developed the analytical model for the study and collaborated closely with ADB's team to bring new insights and directions and we are grateful for this professional collaboration.

Brajesh Panth, Ayako Inagaki, Robert Guild, and Rana Hasan provided valuable guidance to the study. We thank Shamit Chakravarti, Lynette Perez, Yumiko Yamakawa, and Sakiko Tanaka in ADB's Southeast Asia Human and Social Development Division and Paul Vandenberg and Elisabetta Gentile from the Economic Research and Regional Cooperation Department for providing inputs at various stages of the study and Sophea Mar, Sutarum Wiryono, Vinh Ngo from ADB resident missions in Cambodia, Indonesia, and Viet Nam, respectively, for their valuable support and country-level consultations. Iris Miranda, Sheela Rances, and Dorothy Geronimo from ADB, and Jannis Hoh, Shivin Kohli, and Anna Lim from AlphaBeta provided timely coordination of meetings and activities during the study. We thank April Gallega for coordinating the editing of the reports for publication and Mike Cortes for the cover designs.

The study would not have been possible if not for the leadership of senior government and industry representatives and senior members of the academia in the respective countries. We were heartened to note the high level of interest on the topic of 4IR. In each of the countries, there are already several important initiatives underway to enable industry and companies to move toward application of 4IR. The study was closely coordinated with senior government and industry participants, specifically on the selection of the two sectors for detailed study for each of the countries. The emerging findings of the study were shared in country level workshops. Senior officials and key counterparts consulted are listed at the end of each country report.

We look forward to discussions in taking forward the study's policy recommendations.

Shanti Jagannathan
Principal Education Specialist
Sustainable Development
and Climate Change Department

Sameer Khatiwada
Social Sector Specialist
South East Asia Department

Abbreviations

4IR	Industry 4.0 or Fourth Industrial Revolution
ADB	Asian Development Bank
AI	artificial intelligence
ASEAN	Association of Southeast Asian Nations
BPO	business process outsourcing
EdTech	education technology
F&B	food and beverage
GDP	Gross domestic product
IBPAP	IT and Business Process Association of the Philippines
ICT	information and communication technology
ILO	International Labour Organization
IT	information technology
IT-BPO	information technology and business process outsourcing
ITM	industry transformation map
MSMEs	micro, small, and medium-sized enterprises
OECD	Organisation for Economic Co-operation and Development
R&D	research and development
TESDA	Technical Education and Skills Development Authority (Philippines)
TVET	technical and vocational education and training
UNCTAD	United Nations Conference on Trade and Development
UNESCO	United Nations Educational, Scientific and Cultural Organization
WEF	World Economic Forum

Executive Summary

Background to and Rationale for the Study

The future of jobs is at the heart of development in Asia and the Pacific. This makes preparing workers with the right skills and capabilities for the future central to the Asian Development Bank (ADB) portfolio for technical and vocational education and training (TVET) and skills development. In recent years, disruptive technologies have unsettled labor markets, intensifying worries of extensive job losses as a result of automation and of economies in the region losing their comparative advantage where this is based on low labor costs. Policymakers are concerned about how well developing countries can transition effectively to Industry 4.0, or the Fourth Industrial Revolution (4IR). To better understand the implications of 4IR on the future of jobs and to assess the readiness of education and training institutions to prepare for future labor markets, ADB undertook a study that seeks to capture the anticipated transformations on jobs, tasks, and skills, and to outline policy directions to prepare the workforce for future jobs.

Scope of the Study

The study covered Cambodia, Indonesia, the Philippines, and Viet Nam and included the following features:

(i) It focused on two industries in each country deemed important for growth, employment, and 4IR: tourism and garments in Cambodia, food and beverage (F&B) manufacturing and automotive manufacturing in Indonesia, information technology and business process outsourcing (IT-BPO) and electronics in the Philippines, and agro-processing and logistics in Viet Nam. The table shows the economic importance of each industry in each economy.

(ii) The study includes a survey of employers in the chosen industries, a modeling exercise to estimate job displacement and gains, a survey of training institutions on their readiness for 4IR, and analysis of data from online job portals from each country to assess trends in skills demand.

(iii) The policy landscape was assessed, based on benchmarks derived from international trends and experiences, for its ability to harness the potential of Industry 4.0 to increase productivity, facilitate skills development, and incentivize industry.

(iv) Recommendations suggest how to strengthen policy approaches to 4IR, especially the investments needed for skills and training, new approaches to deliver them, and strategies and actions to enhance the readiness of each country's workforce for 4IR.

Overview of Industry Economic Importance

Industry	Country	Employment[a] (%)	GDP[b] (%)	Exports[c] (%)
Tourism	Cambodia	26.4 (2019)[d]	26.4 (2019)[d]	N/A
Garment manufacturing[e]	Cambodia	11.2 (2018)[f]	17.8 (2017)	67.5 (2016)
F&B manufacturing	Indonesia	4.0 (2015)	6.6 (2019)	4.1 (2017)
Automotive manufacturing	Indonesia	0.1 (2015)[g]	2.0 (2019)[h]	4.1 (2018)[i]
IT-BPO	Philippines	2.7 (2016)[j]	6.0 (2018)[k]	10–15 of global market
Electronics	Philippines	2.0 (2018)	5.0 (2018)	Electronic goods 10.5 (2018); parts and components for electronic and electrical goods 31.5 (2018)[l]
Agro-processing	Viet Nam	5.8 (2016)	15.0 (2018)	Food products 2.7; textiles 16.3 (2016)
Logistics[n]	Viet Nam	3.3 (2017)	2.9 (2017)	1.8 (2016)

GDP = gross domestic product, F&B = food and beverage, IT-BPO = information technology and business process outsourcing, N/A = not available.

Note: Economic data are based on the latest available information, from 2015 to 2018.

[a] Where available, based on data from national statistics offices or International Labour Organization (ILO) data.
[b] Where available, based on data from national statistics offices.
[c] Where available, based on data from World Bank. World Integrated Trade Solutions Database (accessed 1 December 2019).
[d] World Travel and Tourism Council. 2020. *Travel and Tourism Economic Impact 2019*.
[e] Industry classification "textiles and clothing."
[f] Estimate based on ILO. 2018. *Cambodia Garment and Footwear Sector Bulletin*.
[g] Industry classification "motor vehicles, trailers, and semi-trailers."
[h] Industry classification "transportation equipment industry."
[i] United Nations Conference on Trade and Development Statistics Database (UNCTADStat) for "road vehicles" (accessed 1 December 2019).
[j] As IT-BPO cuts across several industries, data provided by the IT and Business Process Association of the Philippines is used, rather than computing employment from national statistics.
[k] Bureau for Employers' Activities and ILO. 2017. *ASEAN in Transformation: How Technology Is Changing Jobs and Enterprises—The Philippines Country Brief*. Geneva.
[l] UNCTADStat (accessed 1 December 2019).
[n] Tran, T. 2019. Vietnam's Food Processing Industry: Promising For Foreign Investors. *SEAvestor*.
[m] Industry classification "transportation and storage."

Source: Asian Development Bank and AlphaBeta.

The COVID-19 Effect

The study was undertaken and completed prior to the spread of coronavirus disease (COVID-19), which has caused unprecedented disruptions to labor markets and to the activities of the workforce across the world. This study's policy recommendations and strategies to strengthen widespread digital capabilities, online/distant learning, digital platforms, education technology, and simulation-based learning have become all the more relevant in the aftermath of COVID-19. The key approaches discussed in the report bear great relevance to the current context of countries experiencing nationwide closures of schools and training institutes. The expectation is also that, after COVID-19, there will be operating procedures that constitute a "new normal" that entails far more digital capabilities in the workplace. Hence, the findings of this study and the follow-on policy directions are very timely and crucial to facilitating a sustainable COVID-19 recovery strategy.

The eight sectors chosen for the study across the four countries have been adversely affected. In F&B and agro-processing, the expectation is that there will be lasting shifts in consumer behavior in responding to COVID-19. Food retailers are likely to scale up e-commerce. The logistics part of the sector—storing, transporting, and delivering—is likely to become more tech-oriented, calling for new skills and talent.

Tourism worldwide has more or less ground to a halt as a result of COVID-19. The scale of cancellations and other disruptions calls for greater use of digital tools and capabilities to orient the sector to a future world.

Workers in the garment industry have suffered massive layoffs as factories are closing down owing to internal supply constraints and external demand shocks as a result of COVID-19.

In the IT-BPO sector, there have been widespread disruptions to business operations as a result of COVID-19; however, the expectation is that there will be lasting shifts in business practices that embody greater digital collaborative tools with cybersecurity and management following the pandemic.

In the auto and electronics industries, recovery after COVID-19 will entail embracing digital supply chains and launching digital sales and marketing initiatives.

The logistics sector more broadly is expected to experience a significant upswing after COVID-19 arising from the growth of e-commerce and the changing nature of retail business owing to the pandemic. A recovery strategy will entail embracing digital supply chains and launching digital sales and marketing initiatives. Hence, upskilling and reskilling on 4IR-related occupations is even more urgent for the revival of the economy and economic stimulus needed after COVID-19.

The study does not address the implications of COVID-19 in these countries; however, the policy directions and recommended future investments for higher-order skills, particularly in the digital domain, are eminently suitable for the countries to reimagine new beginnings for the sectors discussed.

Key findings from the study are as follows:

(i) **4IR will bring both job displacement and job gains.**
   (a) 4IR technologies will eliminate some jobs—displacing, for example, up to a third of the agro-processing workforce in Viet Nam. At the same time, 4IR technologies may generate new labor demand. The study estimates a positive net effect in all sectors analyzed: 39% for garments and 2% for tourism in Cambodia, 14% for F&B manufacturing and 1% for automotive manufacturing in Indonesia, 11% for IT-BPO and 10% for electronics in the Philippines, and 34% for agro-processing and 12% for logistics in Viet Nam. The study warns that many displaced workers will likely lack the skills they need to move seamlessly into new jobs without adequate and timely investments in skills development.
   (b) Significant productivity improvements are expected from 4IR technologies in all the sectors analyzed. However, the share of employers who believe the productivity impact of 4IR technologies may be greater than 25% within 5 years varies by sector and country: 12% for garments and 19% for tourism in Cambodia, 52% for F&B manufacturing and 76% for automotive manufacturing in Indonesia, 63% for IT-BPO and 55% for electronics in the Philippines, and 31% for agro-processing and 41% for logistics in Viet Nam. Employers' estimates of 4IR potential correlate strongly with their reported understanding of these technologies. Cambodian employers, for example, had a limited understanding of 4IR technologies and also expected limited benefits. A clear policy implication is the need to educate these firms about 4IR technologies.
   (c) Progress is already substantial in some industries, with 59% of employers in IT-BPO in the Philippines reporting that they had adopted 4IR technologies. However, others lag considerably behind. In Cambodia, just 6% of garment businesses reported implementing any 4IR technologies. These findings highlight how urgent it is to train the workforce to keep pace with change where it is rapid and to support the adoption of 4IR technologies where it lags.

(ii) **4IR could have important implications for gender and inclusiveness.**
   (a) Likely gender impacts of job displacement vary significantly by country and industry. According to IT-BPO employers surveyed in the Philippines, for example, manual and administrative jobs are likely to see the largest employment losses with 4IR adoption, as technical jobs enjoy the largest increases. As it is mostly women who hold administrative jobs in this industry, 4IR poses a real risk of throwing the IT-BPO industry into a gender imbalance if female administrators are not adequately retrained. Elsewhere, job displacement is more likely to affect males in logistics in Viet Nam and females in garments in Cambodia.
   (b) Manual workers in particular face extensive displacement as a result of the adoption of 4IR technologies. A strong focus on retraining programs is required to ensure the welfare of these workers.
   (c) Micro, small, and medium-sized enterprises may struggle to fund their adoption of 4IR technologies, and rural residents may lack access to training programs to help them prepare for 4IR.

(iii) **Job tasks will shift from routine, physical tasks to higher-order tasks with 4IR.**
   (a) The prevalence of jobs involving routine physical tasks is expected to decline as jobs that entail analytical and nonroutine tasks proliferate. The study indicates an increase in time spent on analytical tasks across all industries and countries, with time spent on routine

physical tasks decreasing significantly by 2030. Technology will be able to automate routine physical and interpersonal tasks, leaving humans to focus on more complex and novel tasks that require problem-solving abilities. In IT-BPO, for example, this can involve call center agents responding to unique customer queries and problems, or IT operators scrambling to plug a new security breach.
(b) Skills for "evaluation, judgment, and decision-making" are predicted to become the most important ones in all industries except tourism, which will demand "written and verbal communication," and electronics, which will demand "numeracy." It is generally expected that management skills will become less important in relative terms, mainly because 4IR technologies are expected to simplify the monitoring of workers.

(iv) **Shortages of skills at the required proficiency need to be addressed in all industries.**
(a) While preparing the workforce for 4IR, it is important to address skills shortages and lack of preparation for the workplace. Despite close engagement with industry, significant mismatches in perceptions on skills preparation separate employers and training institutions. While 96% of training institutions in Indonesia believed that their graduates were well prepared for work, for example, only 33% of employers in F&B manufacturing agreed, along with only 30% of employers in automotive manufacturing. In Cambodia, almost 90% of employers reported that graduates were inadequately educated and/or trained before being hired. Large shares of employers in other countries similarly reported that they did not find graduates adequately prepared for entry-level positions.
(b) Employers in all eight surveyed industries stressed the importance of training and skills development. Together, these industries could need training programs sufficient to raise 169 million workers' skills from competence adequate for 2018 to competence demanded in an equivalent or replacement skill in 2030. Although on-the-job training will be critical to skills development in all industries, education and training institutions will still need to prepare graduates better for entry-level positions.

(v) **Training institutions in all four countries need to prepare for the challenges of 4IR.**
(a) Encouragingly, most training institutions reported high engagement with businesses. However, some may struggle to keep pace with the rate of change in skills demand. For example, almost half of training institutions surveyed review and update their curricula less than annually, and again only about half provide information on job market conditions to their students.
(b) Over half of training institutions reported that they already had dedicated programs for 4IR skills, and an even higher share in all four countries reported plans to develop or expand programs for 4IR by 2025. While this is an encouraging trend, it is critical to assess the quality of such training, as well as its relevance and alignment with employer needs. Structured needs assessments for 4IR training are needed, as 63%–90% of training institutions surveyed in the four countries stated that they needed additional financial and technical support for 4IR skills development.

(vi) **Courses and training delivery have begun to change but further transformation is needed.**
(a) The study found promising trends in training institutions, which self-reported classroom teaching and learning adapted for greater assimilation of technology, particularly digital training. Over half the surveyed training institutions run digital programs for improving digital literacy. Over 70% of them use online self-learning tools, though Viet Nam lags,

with just 45% of institutions reporting using this technology. The deployment of advanced technologies remains limited, however, with only 4%–19% of training institutions in the four countries having adopted virtual learning platforms. The quality of these new tools has not yet been ascertained, nor have the standards maintained in their use.

(b) Training institutions have a strong focus on instructor and teacher assessment, but teacher and trainer exposure to the workplace is limited. While over 80% of surveyed training institutions conduct annual or semiannual performance reviews, fewer institutions ensure that teachers have on-the-job time devoted to gaining practical knowledge and new teaching techniques.

(vii) **4IR policies and strategies are heading in the right direction but need active implementation.**

(a) The starting point for successful implementation is to ensure that aims are both clear and realistic, and that skills policy integrates closely with the overall 4IR strategy. Only Cambodia and Indonesia currently have clearly articulated visions for 4IR, though Viet Nam is developing its National Strategy for Industry 4.0. Across all four countries, 4IR strategy is integrated in a limited way with the national skills and employment strategy.

(b) One common challenge for all four countries lies in raising awareness of which skills are in demand. Large shares of employers reported a lack of suitable training programs for their workers, and workers often do not know what courses to take. Both findings point to weak understanding of the opportunities available in each country for acquiring new skills, or "reskilling," despite government efforts to catalyze these. A further common challenge is to incentivize employers and workers to actively develop skills. Surveys of training institutions also highlighted that training courses would be taken up more readily if they were more affordable.

(c) Policy assessments conducted in this study found that all four focus countries had attempted to revamp their curricula, with Indonesia arguably having the strongest 4IR focus. However, rigid training systems mean that curriculum reform can be painfully slow. In addition, policy assessments and national consultations highlighted that all four countries maintained a strong emphasis on traditional qualifications attained through the education system or competency assessments, with little consideration of previous work experience or the skills thus acquired.

(d) There is little evidence of strong government focus on expanding efforts to include underserved groups and ensure their access to better opportunities in the labor market, let alone train them in preparation for 4IR. It is the private sector and nongovernment organizations that undertake most such programs. In addition, social protection mechanisms are limited even for regular staff, and even weaker for flexible workers—those who work on demand and constitute a rapidly expanding labor segment in each country.

Key Recommendations and the Way Forward

Several recommendations applicable to all four focus countries are offered to address current gaps in policy, make implementation more effective, and better prepare for 4IR:

(i) **Develop 4IR transformation road maps for key sectors.** To better integrate 4IR strategy with required skillsets, all four countries should consider developing industry transformation maps, as has Singapore, to provide information on technology impacts, career pathways, the skills required for various occupations, and the reskilling options available. Industry-specific road maps in this report could be useful starting points.

(ii) **Develop industry-led TVET programs targeting skills for 4IR.** Courses and credentials for 4IR in each focus industry need to be developed to strengthen TVET programs and thus build on existing mechanisms for industry engagement. Generation, an independent nonprofit founded by the global management consulting firm McKinsey & Company, is a good example of an industry-led program. Of the more than 30,000 people who have graduated from its programs in 13 countries, 81% were employed by 3 months after graduation and earning salaries 2–6 times higher than previously. While the program covers a broad range of occupations, it includes a strong focus on developing skills for 4IR technologies, including digital marketing and the development of automated processes using robotics.

(iii) **Upgrade training delivery through 4IR technology in classrooms and training facilities.** Technology adoption in the classroom for 4IR appears to be limited in all four countries. Greater deployment of new technologies such as virtual reality, augmented reality, and virtual simulation would strengthen workforce readiness. Given the substantial need for on-the-job training for new and upgraded skills, digital platforms should be explored to deliver skills training. These new approaches need to become routine in high schools, TVET institutions, polytechnics, and higher education institutes. It would be valuable to prepare a systematic suite of 4IR methodologies for use in training delivery.

(iv) **Develop flexible and modular skills certification programs.** Countries should develop flexible skills certification programs that recognize skills attainment outside of traditional education channels. A good example is the Malaysian Skills Certification Program, which grants skills certificates to workers who lack formal educational qualifications but have obtained relevant knowledge, experience, and skills in the workplace. Given large requirements for new and upgraded skills, industry-led certification of workers' gradual mastery of skills is required.

(v) **Formulate new approaches and measures to strengthen inclusion and social protection under 4IR.** This should cover training for three types of workers—entry level, those at risk of job displacement, and those who need upskilling—through such modern delivery mechanisms as digital platforms and industry-recognized credentials. One approach is through online learning channels such as those encouraged and supported by the Ministry of Higher Education in Malaysia, with universities creating massive open courses mandated to be made available online to the general public. Another is to target skills development programs for specific underserved groups. Still another is to provide financial incentives for employers to train specific underserved communities, as does the Career-Up Josei-Kin program in Japan, which subsidizes employers to train individuals not on regular contracts. Cost–benefit analyses are recommended for several policy options with the potential to improve social protection for flexible workers; the most promising schemes should be piloted to test their broader applicability. Worth exploring are policy approaches to enhance income security for those who work on demand. In Australia, for example, workers on short-term contracts are entitled to an increment of 25% per hour over what a worker receives doing the same job on a regular basis. Another approach is to work with key employers to champion corporate policies mandating income stability for flexible workers.

(vi) **Implement an incentive scheme for firms to train employees for 4IR.** Despite the substantial productivity gains 4IR technologies could bring about, employer training rates remain low in all countries. This is the result of a number of market failures relating to information asymmetries around the benefits of training, as well as weak incentives for employers. A set of support programs should be developed to encourage firms to invest in 4IR training for their workers. A good start would be to prepare guidelines and incentive frameworks supported by robust cost–benefit analysis.

While these recommendations apply to all eight focus industries across the four countries, a set of unique priorities should be considered for each industry when implementing the respective policy actions. For example, firms in the manufacturing industries tend to have more limited knowledge of relevant 4IR technologies than do firms in service industries. The gender impacts of the 4IR job displacement also vary significantly by industry, as do some of the key skills that will become more important (as highlighted earlier). Taking account of these different industry nuances will be crucial in developing effective industry-specific programs.

CHAPTER 1
The Industry 4.0 Skills Challenge

This chapter investigates demand for skills driven by technology adoption under the Fourth Industrial Revolution (4IR) and their supply in selected industries in four focus countries: Cambodia, Indonesia, the Philippines, and Viet Nam. The analysis taps employer surveys and interviews, online job board data, and national labor market statistics.

The returns to businesses of implementing 4IR technologies could be large. In automotive manufacturing in Indonesia, for example, 76% of employers believe productivity improvements from 4IR technologies could exceed 25% over the next 5 years. Employers' estimates of the potential of 4IR correlate strongly with their reported understanding of these technologies. Cambodian employers, for example, revealed only limited understanding of 4IR technologies and similarly expected only limited potential benefits. A clear policy implication of this is the need to educate such firms about 4IR technologies.

In all industries, 4IR could have transformative impacts on jobs and skills. Analysis to 2030 shows that, despite widespread concerns over significant automation and loss of jobs associated with 4IR, the net impact on jobs in all analyzed industries is likely to be positive, with more jobs created than displaced. However, there are no guarantees that displaced workers will be able to move seamlessly into these new jobs, as they will likely lack the needed skills. In agro-processing in Viet Nam, for example, 4IR technologies could displace up to one-third of the workforce.

Employers in all eight analyzed industries stressed the importance of training and skills development. Together, they could need an additional 169 million person-trainings by 2030.[1] In all industries, on-the-job training will be crucial to expanded skills development, but education and training institutions still need to better prepare graduates for entry-level positions.

Industry 4.0 and Its Relevance for Cambodia, Indonesia, the Philippines, and Viet Nam

4IR refers to a range of new technologies that have profound effects on the workplace. The term was first applied to data exchange technologies used in manufacturing. However, it has now acquired a broader meaning in reference to technologies applied across all sectors that combine the physical, digital, and biological worlds.[2] These technologies notably include cyberphysical systems, the Internet of Things, Artificial Intelligence (AI), cloud computing, and cognitive computing.

---

[1] One person-training trains one worker in one skill from the average competence required by his or her occupation in his or her industry in 2018 to the competence required in 2030.

[2] K. Schwab. 2017. *The Fourth Industrial Revolution*. New York: Currency.

4IR is very different from previous industrial revolutions in both scope and technologies (Figure 1). The first industrial revolution, in the 18th century, was marked by a transition from hand production and the use of draft animals to mechanization through hydro and steam power. The second industrial revolution occurred in the 19th century and featured the introduction of extensive railroad and telegraph networks to speed the transfer of people, goods, and ideas, combined with factory electrification and mass production assembly lines. The third industrial revolution, in the late 20th century, is often called the digital revolution, as it featured the introduction of computers, the internet, robots and automation, and electronics. 4IR builds on these past industrial revolutions but includes a far broader array of technologies with applicability across all industries. In this regard, it is fundamentally different from past industrial revolutions in its potential implications for economies and employment.

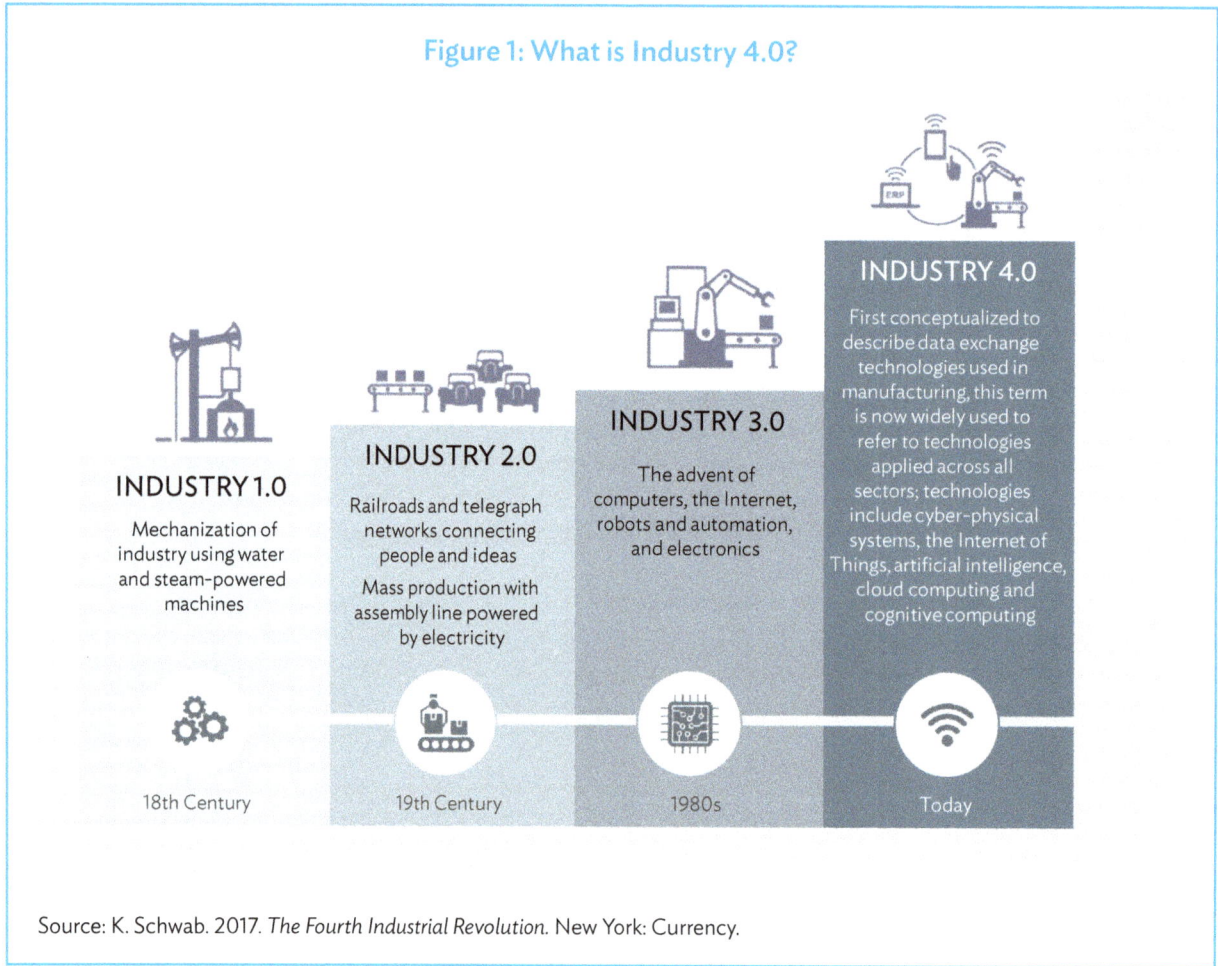

Figure 1: What is Industry 4.0?

Source: K. Schwab. 2017. *The Fourth Industrial Revolution.* New York: Currency.

What could 4IR mean for Cambodia, Indonesia, the Philippines, and Viet Nam? In an International Labour Organization (ILO) study in 2017, Philippine enterprises perceived technological advance to be the second biggest economic opportunity in the period to 2025, second only to a rise in domestic demand.[3] According to the Central Institute for Economic Management, 4IR technology adoption could

---

[3] Bureau for Employers' Activities and ILO (International Labour Organization). 2017. ASEAN in Transformation: How Technology is Changing Jobs and Enterprises—The Philippines Country Brief. Geneva: ILO.

increase Viet Nam's gross domestic product (GDP) by $29 billion–$62 billion by 2030, equal to a rise of 7%–16% over 2018, as a result of increased productivity and employment opportunities. More broadly, a study by McKinsey & Company in 2018 showed, for example, that early 4IR adopters in the Association of Southeast Asian Nations (ASEAN) had demonstrated high productivity gains of 10%–50%.[4]

Given the potentially transformative nature of 4IR technology adoption, concerns understandably arise over its impact on employment. Most of these revolve around fears that 4IR could bring mass unemployment as workers are replaced by machines or lack the skills to work effectively alongside 4IR technologies or transition into the new jobs that emerge.

The rapid pace at which technology is being developed and adopted is making it difficult to understand how the skills landscape is likely to change under 4IR. This is making it inappropriate to use traditional approaches to assessing skills gaps, which often rely on time-consuming processes to collect data that quickly become outdated. This study explores a new approach to understanding the labor market implications of 4IR that aims to address gaps in previous studies. Some of the key design aspects are as follows:

(i) **Use of local data.** This study uses a variety of local data sources, including national labor force surveys, World Bank surveys under its Skills Measurement Program, and surveys of over 500 local businesses in focus industries across the four countries.

(ii) **Use of current market information.** Given how rapidly labor markets change, existing labor market surveys can quickly become obsolete. This study therefore uses information on skills profiles for jobs currently advertised on online portals in each of the four countries. The job portal chosen for each country is the one the selected industry uses most frequently, based on its number of job listings.[5]

(iii) **Focus on not just demand but also supply.** Much past research has examined changes in occupations and skills only in relation to 4IR. This study goes further by examining the supply landscape—including the volume and types of training required, such as on-the-job training and short professional courses—and by conducting surveys of training institutions in each of the four countries, to understand the degree to which they currently address shifts in demand for skills seen elsewhere in the analysis. Further, the study surveyed more than 300 training institutions across the four countries to gauge their understanding of and readiness for 4IR; current and planned skills training provision for 4IR; and general attitudes and approaches to staff training, industry engagement, and government policy and regulations.[6]

Industry Selection

Eight industries were chosen for the analysis of 4IR implications for skills demand and supply. They were selected using a two-step methodology:

(i) shortlisting industries that each government has prioritized for future growth or for 4IR application and

---

[4] I. Arbulu et al. 2018. *Industry 4.0: Reinvigorating ASEAN Manufacturing for the Future*. McKinsey & Company. 8 February. https://www.mckinsey.com/business-functions/operations/our-insights/industry-4-0-reinvigorating-asean-manufacturing-for-the-future.

[5] The job portals were Pelprek in Cambodia, Karir in Indonesia, Bestjobs.ph in the Philippines, and Vietnam Works in Viet Nam. Only one job portal was chosen per country to avoid the risk of counting the same job listing more than once, as employers typically advertise jobs on more than one portal.

[6] Surveys covered 51 institutions in Cambodia, 72 in Indonesia, 120 in the Philippines, and 74 in Viet Nam.

(ii) scoring and ranking shortlisted industries according to the following criteria:
   (a) How significant is the industry's contribution to the country's employment?
   (b) Has it recently exhibited strong employment growth?
   (c) Are its exports internationally competitive?
   (d) Is 4IR relevant to the industry?
   (e) Are data available for industry analysis?

Industry selection was then tested with various stakeholders during country consultations conducted in July 2019. Using this process, eight industries were selected for analysis, two in each focus country.

Cambodia

(i) **Garment manufacturing.** Garment manufacturing comprises sewing, cutting, making, processing, repairing, finishing, assembling, or otherwise preparing any piece of apparel or accessory designed to be worn by an individual. It includes items such as clothing, hats, gloves, handbags, hosiery, and neckties. According to latest data from the Cambodia's National Institute for Statistics, the garment industry contributed 17.8% to the country's GDP in 2017.[7] This contribution has grown by almost 8% annually since 2012. Textiles are Cambodia's major export, accounting for 67.5% of exports in 2016, followed by footwear at 8.2%. The country has a strong comparative advantage in garment and footwear production. During country consultations, stakeholders debated whether Cambodia should diversify out of garments for future economic growth. They reached consensus that Cambodia should aim to depend less on low-cost production by moving toward production with higher value added, and that 4IR technologies could facilitate this transition. A key barrier noted to the successful implementation of 4IR was the current low skills level of workers.

(ii) **Tourism.** The tourism industry covers a broad range of products and services for tourists at different stages of travel and tourism, with a particular focus on hotels and restaurants. According to the World Travel & Tourism Council, the industry employs around 26.4% of workers and contributes a similar share of GDP for Cambodia, and was growing at 8.6% per year prior to the coronavirus disease pandemic.[8] The government is strongly pushing this industry to adopt and reap the benefits of digital technologies, using new hospitality and tourism management technologies such as tour guide apps, online and automatic check-in systems, and inventory management software.

Indonesia

(i) **Food and beverage manufacturing.** The food and beverage (F&B) manufacturing industry comprises all businesses that process, package, or distribute food—fresh, prepared, or packaged—and including beverages, both alcoholic and not. It is a major contributor to Indonesian employment, with over 4.5 million workers, or almost 4% of all employment in 2015 and over a quarter of employment in all processing industries. Industry employment grew rapidly, by over 10%, from 2013 to 2015. As a result, the industry is a major locus for economic activity, contributing 6.6% to GDP in 2018—a contribution that has been growing by 8.5% annually since 2015. The industry is a key priority in Indonesia's National Industrial Development Master Plan, 2015–2035 and, more importantly for this study, one of the five priority industries in Making Indonesia 4.0, the country's Industry 4.0 development strategy. Consultations with various ministries and industry associations revealed a strong push to further

---

[7] Government of Cambodia, National Institute of Statistics. 2020. https://www.nis.gov.kh/index.php/km/.
[8] World Travel & Tourism Council. 2020. *Travel and Tourism Economic Impact 2019.*

develop this industry for greater export competitiveness. In particular, stakeholders articulated an ambition for Indonesia to be the ASEAN F&B powerhouse by 2030. 4IR could be key to achieving this, as it offers potentially high productivity gains.

(ii) **Automotive manufacturing.** The automotive manufacturing industry comprises a wide range of businesses involved in the design, development, manufacturing, marketing, and selling of motor vehicles. Like F&B manufacturing, the automotive manufacturing industry is one of the five priority industries of Making Indonesia 4.0. The broader manufacturing of transport equipment is a key priority in Indonesia's National Industrial Development Master Plan, 2015–2035. Government and industry stakeholders expressed a shared desire to move up the value chain by 2030 and expand into new product segments, such as electrical vehicles and associated ecosystem components such as batteries and charging stations. Employment in the automotive industry, while significantly smaller than that in F&B manufacturing, grew at a similarly rapid pace, of 7.6% annually, from 2013 to 2015. The transportation equipment industry contributed almost 2% of Indonesian GDP in 2018, growing by 4.1% annually since 2015, and accounted for close to 4% of exports in 2017, according to the World Bank. Micro, small, and medium-sized enterprises (MSMEs) play a major role in this industry: 70% of enterprises in the automotive industry are MSMEs that supply parts to large manufacturers.

Philippines

(i) **Business process outsourcing.** Business process outsourcing (BPO) is the contracting of support business activities and functions to a third-party provider. Information technology and business process outsourcing (IT-BPO) uses IT to deliver these contracted services, such as through call centers, knowledge process outsourcing and back offices, animation, software development, game development, engineering design, and medical transcription. The BPO industry in the Philippines has grown rapidly since the beginning of the 20th century, averaging a growth rate estimated at 17%–18% (footnote 3). Further reflecting this growth, the BPO contribution to GDP increased from less than 1% in 2000 to 6% in 2015 (footnote 3). An abundant pool of service-minded and English-speaking workers, supportive government policies, and the presence of business associations have enabled the industry's rapid development. According to the IT & Business Process Association of the Philippines, the industry contributed 2.7% of employment in 2016 and held a 10%–15% share of the global IT-BPO market. Information and communication technology (ICT) services, much of which fall under IT-BPO in the Philippines, is the industry that Philippine students, both male and female, most desire to enter, with 25.7% of male students and 18.5% of female students surveyed by the ILO in 2017 expressing this desire—almost double the share favoring hotels and restaurants, the second most desirable industry. IT-BPO faces great potential for disruption from 4IR, however, with 89% of Philippine BPO jobs at high risk of replacement through automation (footnote 3).

(ii) **Electronics manufacturing.** Electronics manufacturing includes businesses that design, manufacture, test, distribute, and provide return or repair services for electronic components and assemblies for original equipment manufacturers.[9] According to the latest available national statistics, the electronics manufacturing industry took up 2% of employment in 2015.[10] According to the United Nations Conference on Trade and Development Statistics Database (UNCTADStat), electronics contributed 10.5% of Philippine exports in 2018, making the country the fifth largest exporter of electronics in ASEAN and the 19th largest worldwide.

---

[9] B. Lüthje. 2002. Electronics Contract Manufacturing: Global Production and the International Division of Labor in the Age of the Internet. *Industry and Innovation* 9 (3).

[10] Philippines Statistics Authority. 2018. Summary Statistics for Manufacturing Establishments. *OpenSTAT*.

Machinery and electronics jointly made up 60.6% of Philippine exports in 2017, with the country enjoying comparative advantages in both product groups. The government has designated electronics manufacturing as a key industry and prioritized it for 4IR technology adoption under the Inclusive Innovation Industrial Strategy of the Department of Trade and Industry, along with aerospace parts, agriculture, automotive manufacturing, construction, furniture, garments, iron and steel, IT-BPO, and shipbuilding.[11] Country consultations revealed a push by both government and industry to shift electronics manufacturing further up the value chain, from manufacturing parts toward full-fledged production and assembly centers. There is already nascent collaboration between industry, the government, and education institutions, but stakeholders voiced a need for a better understanding of skills impacts and priorities.

Viet Nam

(i) **Logistics.** Logistics is the process by which resources are acquired, stored, and transported to their final destination. The logistics industry is a significant contributor to employment in Viet Nam. According to the ILO and Viet Nam's *Statistical Yearbook 2017*, the transportation and storage industry contributed 3.3% of employment in that year, with employment in the industry growing by 4.6% annually from 2015 to 2017. However, logistics costs in Viet Nam remain higher than the ASEAN average, with implications for Viet Nam's international competitiveness.[12] Recent data suggest some improvement. The World Bank's Logistics Performance Index,[13] for example, ranks Viet Nam 39th of 160 countries in 2018, an improvement by 25 positions since 2016. 4IR technologies could significantly further improve the performance of the logistics industry. 4IR innovations in product classification, labeling and arrangement, or automatic monitoring of inventory will be crucial as supply chains mature in Viet Nam. This industry is strategically important to growth in other industries, as it is deeply integrated into rapidly growing industries in Viet Nam, including e-commerce.

(ii) **Agro-processing.** Agro-processing is a subset of manufacturing that processes raw materials and intermediate products derived from agriculture. The agro-processing industry encompasses early stages in the production value chain for the manufacture of food products, beverages, tobacco products, textiles, leather and related products, wood and products of wood and cork excluding furniture, and paper and paper products. Data from the General Statistics Office indicate that agro-processing provided 5.8% of employment in Viet Nam in 2016. Actual activities in manufacturing that can be described as agro-processing—by virtue of requiring raw agricultural materials as direct inputs and excluding activities higher up the manufacturing value chain—may provide closer to 4.5% of all jobs, or some 31% of all industrial jobs in Viet Nam.[14] The industry shows strong growth, with employment growing annually by 5.3% on average from 2014 to 2016. Viet Nam's industrial development strategy prioritizes more processing of agricultural products in the period to 2025, in line with its restructuring of the agriculture sector. Agro-processing is currently underdeveloped in Viet Nam but 4IR technologies could enable the country to move up the value chain from a simple focus on primary agriculture. Dairy processing is already emerging as a strong end-to-end value chain, and other agro-processing pursuits are likely to follow.

---

[11] R. M. Aldaba. Industry 4.0: Are We There Yet? I3S Inclusive Innovation Industrial Strategy.
[12] V. L. Dang and G. T. Yeo. 2018. Weighing the Key Factors to Improve Viet Nam's Logistics System. *Asian Journal of Shipping and Logistics*. 34 (4). pp. 308–316; and World Bank. 2014. *Efficient Logistics—A Key to Viet Nam's Competitiveness*. Washington, DC: World Bank.
[13] International Logistics Performance Index. https://lpi.worldbank.org/international/global/2018.
[14] World Bank. 2018. *Vietnam's Future Jobs: Leveraging Mega-Trends for Greater Prosperity* Vol. 3: infographic (Vietnamese).

Relevance of Industry 4.0

Businesses' understanding and adoption of 4IR technologies vary significantly across the focus industries and countries. In Cambodia, the firms' understanding of 4IR technologies and their relevance appears to be particularly low (Figure 2). The adoption of technologies also varies significantly by industry and country, with the highest reported penetration of 4IR technologies currently in IT-BPO in the Philippines (Figure 3). Over half of the employers surveyed in Indonesia, the Philippines, and Viet Nam reported plans to adopt 4IR technologies by 2025.

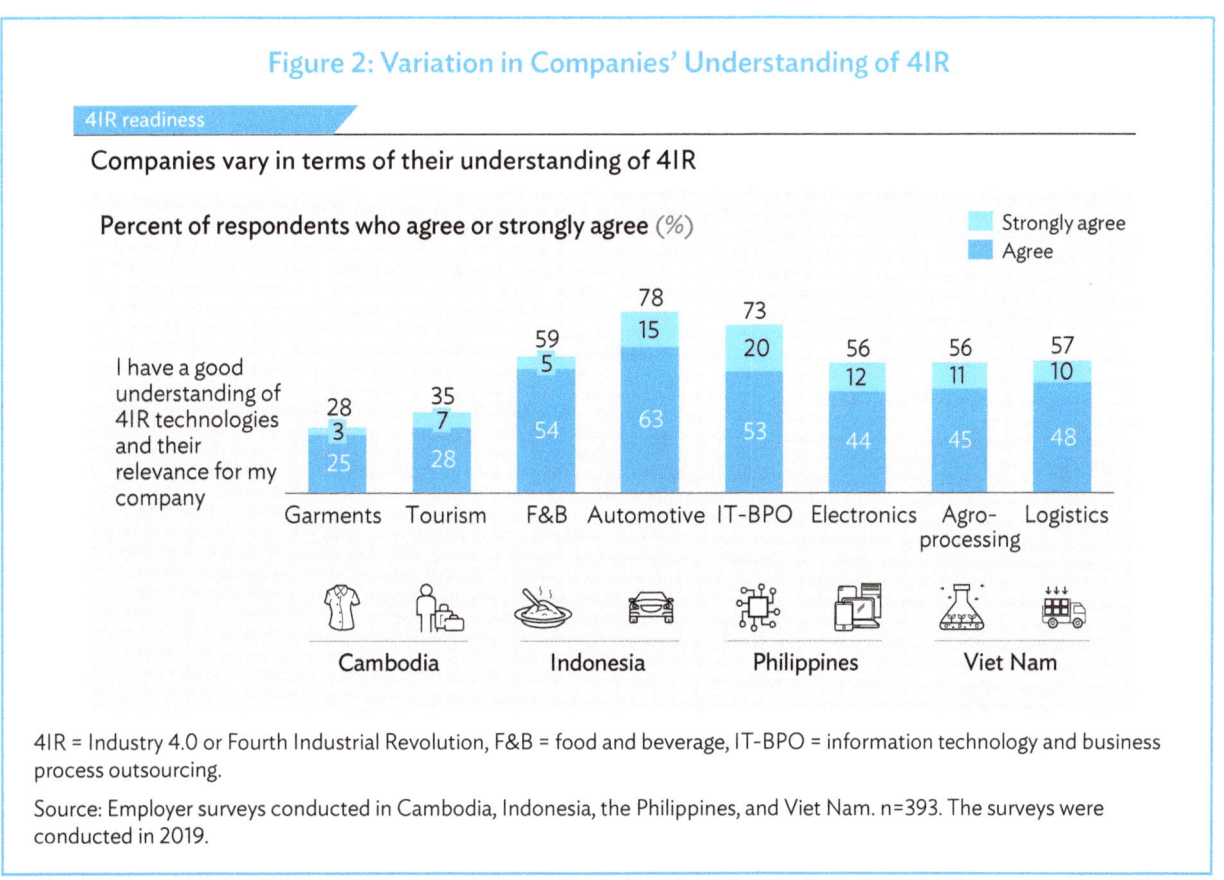

Figure 2: Variation in Companies' Understanding of 4IR

4IR = Industry 4.0 or Fourth Industrial Revolution, F&B = food and beverage, IT-BPO = information technology and business process outsourcing.
Source: Employer surveys conducted in Cambodia, Indonesia, the Philippines, and Viet Nam. n=393. The surveys were conducted in 2019.

Returns to businesses from implementing 4IR technologies could be large. In automotive manufacturing in Indonesia, for example, 76% of employers believe that productivity improvements from 4IR technologies could be greater than 25% over the next 5 years. Over 30% of employers surveyed in Indonesia, the Philippines, and Viet Nam expect productivity increases of over 25% from their application of 4IR technologies (Figure 4). Employers' estimates of the potential of 4IR correlate strongly with their reported understanding of them. Cambodian employers notably had a limited understanding of 4IR technologies—and expected only limited benefits. A clear policy implication is needed to raise awareness of 4IR technologies in these firms.

Figure 3: Sentiment toward the Adoption of 4IR Technologies

4IR readiness

Companies vary in terms of their current and planned adoption of 4IR

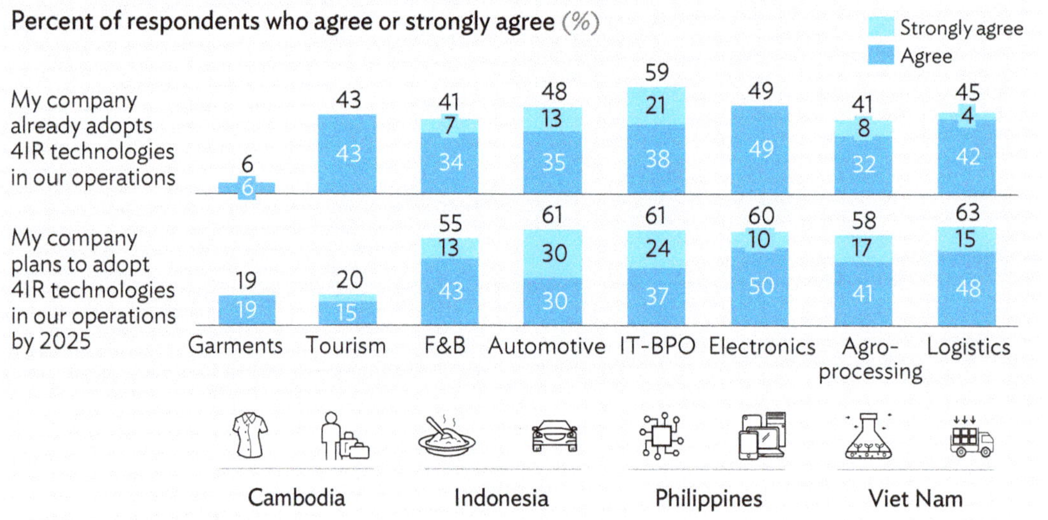

Percent of respondents who agree or strongly agree (%)

Legend: Strongly agree, Agree

My company already adopts 4IR technologies in our operations:
- Garments (Cambodia): 6 (Strongly agree 0, Agree 6)
- Tourism (Cambodia): 43 (Agree 43)
- F&B (Indonesia): 41 (Strongly agree 7, Agree 34)
- Automotive (Indonesia): 48 (Strongly agree 13, Agree 35)
- IT-BPO (Philippines): 59 (Strongly agree 21, Agree 38)
- Electronics (Philippines): 49 (Agree 49)
- Agro-processing (Viet Nam): 41 (Strongly agree 8, Agree 32)
- Logistics (Viet Nam): 45 (Strongly agree 4, Agree 42)

My company plans to adopt 4IR technologies in our operations by 2025:
- Garments: 19 (Agree 19)
- Tourism: 20 (Strongly agree 5, Agree 15)
- F&B: 55 (Strongly agree 13, Agree 43)
- Automotive: 61 (Strongly agree 30, Agree 30)
- IT-BPO: 61 (Strongly agree 24, Agree 37)
- Electronics: 60 (Strongly agree 10, Agree 50)
- Agro-processing: 58 (Strongly agree 17, Agree 41)
- Logistics: 63 (Strongly agree 15, Agree 48)

4IR = Industry 4.0 or Fourth Industrial Revolution, F&B = food and beverage, IT-BPO = information technology and business process outsourcing.

Source: Employer surveys conducted in Cambodia, Indonesia, the Philippines, and Viet Nam. n=393. The surveys were conducted in 2019.

Figure 4: Expected Productivity Improvement from 4IR Technologies in 5 Years

Productivity

The productivity impact from 4IR technologies could be significant in each sector

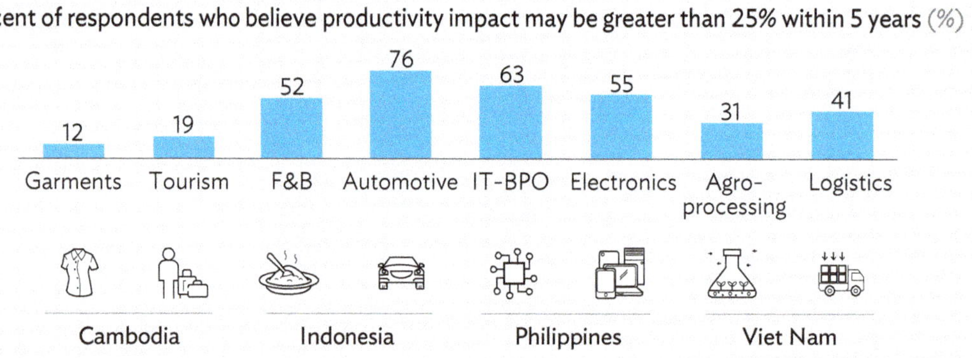

Percent of respondents who believe productivity impact may be greater than 25% within 5 years (%)

- Garments (Cambodia): 12
- Tourism (Cambodia): 19
- F&B (Indonesia): 52
- Automotive (Indonesia): 76
- IT-BPO (Philippines): 63
- Electronics (Philippines): 55
- Agro-processing (Viet Nam): 31
- Logistics (Viet Nam): 41

4IR = Industry 4.0 or Fourth Industrial Revolution, F&B = food and beverage, IT-BPO = information technology and business process outsourcing.

Source: Employer surveys conducted in Cambodia, Indonesia, the Philippines, and Viet Nam. n=393. The surveys were conducted in 2019.

Skills Demand Analysis

Employment Implications

The study examines two factors related to 4IR that influence employment in each of the eight industries:

(i) **Displacement effect.** This is the number of jobs that could be lost to task automation through the application of 4IR technology. Jobs are displaced only if newly automated tasks occupy such a significant portion of worktime, or are so essential to a worker's role, that he or she is no longer needed.

(ii) **Productivity effect.** Sometimes called a scale effect, this refers to productivity improvements and lower production costs as a result of automation. It normally lowers prices for goods and services, thereby unleashing demand for them. To the extent that higher demand requires hiring more workers, it can offset the displacement effect from automation.[15]

Contrary to some perceptions that 4IR will bring mass unemployment, this study informs a more positive assessment that foresees net gains in employment. Net employment may actually rise with the adoption of 4IR in each of the industries studied, as employment linked to productivity gains and a resulting income effect offset displacement effects from 4IR (Figure 5).

Figure 5: Modeled Impact of 4IR on Job Number Change from 2018 to 2030

Jobs

The overall impact of 4IR on jobs is likely to be limited as negative displacement effects are potentially offset by positive income effects

Displacement and income effects of 4IR on jobs, 2018–2030 (% of jobs affected in 2030)

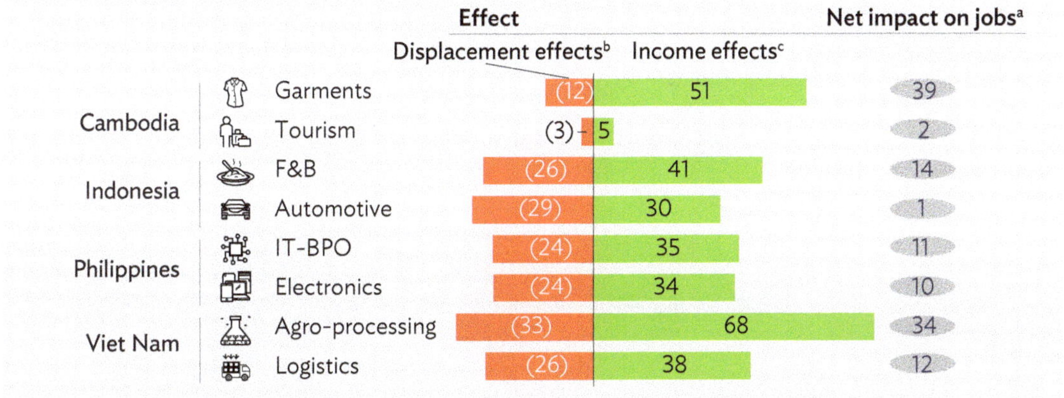

Country	Industry	Displacement effects[b]	Income effects[c]	Net impact on jobs[a]
Cambodia	Garments	(12)	51	39
Cambodia	Tourism	(3)	5	2
Indonesia	F&B	(26)	41	14
Indonesia	Automotive	(29)	30	1
Philippines	IT-BPO	(24)	35	11
Philippines	Electronics	(24)	34	10
Viet Nam	Agro-processing	(33)	68	34
Viet Nam	Logistics	(26)	38	12

( ) = negative, 4IR = Industry 4.0 or Fourth Industrial Revolution, F&B = food and beverage, IT-BPO = information technology and business process outsourcing.

[a] Combination of displacement and income effects.
[b] Job reductions owing to labor substitution effects of 4IR.
[c] Additional labor demand simulated by revenue increases brought about by 4IR-enabled productivity gains.

Source: National employment statistics; World Bank STEP survey 2015; RAND Indonesian Family Life Survey; Employer surveys conducted in the four countries (n=393) in 2019; and AlphaBeta modelling.

---

[15] Automation can also spawn new labor-intensive tasks and jobs, raising demand for labor. New job categories can emerge as 4IR technologies are introduced into production or when a more sophisticated industrial robot is introduced on a factory floor and needs programming. The literature calls this a "reinstatement effect." This effect was not estimated in this analysis, owing to a lack of robust data. For more on reinstatement effects see ADB. 2018. *Asian Development Outlook 2018: How Technology Affects Jobs.* Mandaluyong: ADB.

However, even a net impact on employment that appears to be positive does not mean that 4IR will not lead to large groups of workers losing their jobs. Four factors could affect the theoretical positive income effect:

(i) Displaced workers are not guaranteed a seamless move into new jobs created. This transition may not occur if workers cannot acquire or upgrade to the skills required.
(ii) New jobs may not materialize if there is a lack of suitable skills in the local workforce to support them. Countries' approaches to skills development will be critical to realizing positive labor market outcomes from 4IR.
(iii) As extended time lags may emerge between the implementation of 4IR, job displacement, and the manifestation of productivity benefits, the productivity gains needed to generate the additional income that makes new employment possible may take years to materialize, reducing the positive impact by 2030.
(iv) Companies may absorb some productivity benefits in the form of higher profits in industries without significant competition, or distribute them to the remaining workers as higher wages if the supply of labor is inelastic. Rather than adding employment, productivity benefits could then generate higher returns for existing actors in the market.

The displacement effect varies significantly by industry, affecting up to a third of workers in agro-processing in Viet Nam but probably just 3% of workers in the tourism industry of Cambodia (Box 1).

Box 1: Estimating Employment Changes

This study uses an experimental approach to estimating the impact of Industry 4.0 (4IR) on employment. The core data sources used in this approach are the World Bank's Skills Measurement Program survey,[a] labor force surveys, online job portals, and surveys of employers in focus industries. The approach seeks to understand first how 4IR will likely affect the industry's growth trajectory and then how employment will change with task shifts within occupations.

The growth trajectory of the industry is computed by looking at historic industry growth under a scenario with business as usual and then modeling the impact of 4IR as a productivity shock that generates additional productivity growth. The assumption used for the estimates presented here is that adoption rates for 4IR technology increase to 50% by 2025 and reach 100% by 2030. This approach is not meant to forecast actual or even necessarily realistic adoption of 4IR technology by 2030. Rather, it is a thought experiment to understand the largest possible impact 4IR can have on employment and skills gaps. Productivity shocks and technology adoption rates were obtained from the employer survey and cross-referenced with the broader literature.

Estimating changes in employment across different occupations relies on a detailed analysis of task profiles (Box 2). The analysis calculates changes in the time spent on particular tasks between today and a future in which 4IR has been adopted. Combining this with a breakdown of employment by occupation in the industry, and with the productivity growth estimates referred to above, yields results that show how different occupations may become more frequent in the industry. This part of the analysis mostly relies on data from Skills Measurement Program and labor force surveys.

[a] The Indonesia portion of this study uses the RAND Indonesian Family Life Survey instead: RAND. 2018. *Indonesian Family Life Survey*.

Source: Asian Development Bank and AlphaBeta.

This may have consequences for gender equity. In some industries, notably agro-processing, electronics, tourism, and garments, women are more at risk than men of job loss from automation, whereas in other industries men are at greater risk (Figure 6). Box 2 provides more information on some of the potential equity concerns related to 4IR.

To understand these results, it is important to grasp that technology does not automate whole jobs but, rather, individual tasks or combinations of them. In IT-BPO, for example, AI and big data applications will not replace a customer service agent or IT professional. However, the task of finding solutions for customers, or directing a customer to the right department, will be automated. Replacement occurs only if automation takes over such a high share of job activities that the worker is no longer essential.

Box 2: Equity Concerns Related to Industry 4.0

Although Industry 4.0 (4IR) technologies have the potential to significantly enhance worker productivity and incomes, the following areas have the potential for risks.

Gender equity. 4IR could have significant gender implications. According to employers surveyed in the information technology and business process outsourcing (IT-BPO) industry in the Philippines, for example, manual and administrative jobs are likely to see the largest job losses as a result of 4IR technology adoption, with technical jobs seeing the largest increases. As it is mostly women who hold the administrative jobs in this industry, there is a risk that 4IR technology adoption will shift IT-BPO into a gender imbalance if these women are not adequately retrained to remain in their jobs. In some other industries, particularly logistics in Viet Nam, job displacement is likely to affect men the most; in other industries, notably garments in Cambodia, it is women who will feel the impacts most significantly.

Manual workers. Manual jobs are expected to suffer the greatest displacement from 4IR technologies, with extensive retraining programs required to protect the welfare of workers in these jobs.

Micro, small, and medium-sized enterprises. Past research has shown that micro, small, and medium-sized enterprises (MSMEs) may be significant beneficiaries of 4IR innovations that help them lower the costs and time required to export.[a] However, a large share of employers surveyed in this study cited cost as a key barrier to actual adoption of 4IR technologies—and this could be a particular hurdle for MSMEs. The share of employers citing the cost of technologies varied by sector and country: 57% in garments and 26% in tourism in Cambodia, 45% in F&B manufacturing and 46% in automotive manufacturing in Indonesia, 53% in both IT-BPO and electronics in the Philippines, and 68% in agro-processing and 61% in logistics in Viet Nam. Regulatory issues related to 4IR technologies such as data localization could similarly prove more challenging for MSMEs to handle than larger firms, limiting adoption.

Rural versus urban. Rural inhabitants may find it harder to benefit from 4IR technologies as a result of a lack of training programs nearby. In addition, many rural inhabitants are in jobs that could mean they are less likely to see productivity benefits from 4IR technologies and are more exposed to displacement. This is potentially a big problem in Cambodia, where 77% of workers in rural areas are employed in vulnerable jobs, working under precarious conditions, such as unsafe, unregulated construction sites, and/or suffering uncertain income flows, as do unpaid family workers.[b]

[a] Asia Pacific MSME Trade Coalition. 2017. *Micro-Revolution: The New Stakeholders of Trade in APAC*.
[b] International Labour Organization (ILO). 2015. *Rural Development and Employment Opportunities in Cambodia: How Can a National Employment Policy Contribute Toward Realization of Decent Work in Rural Areas?* Geneva: ILO.

Source: Asian Development Bank and AlphaBeta.

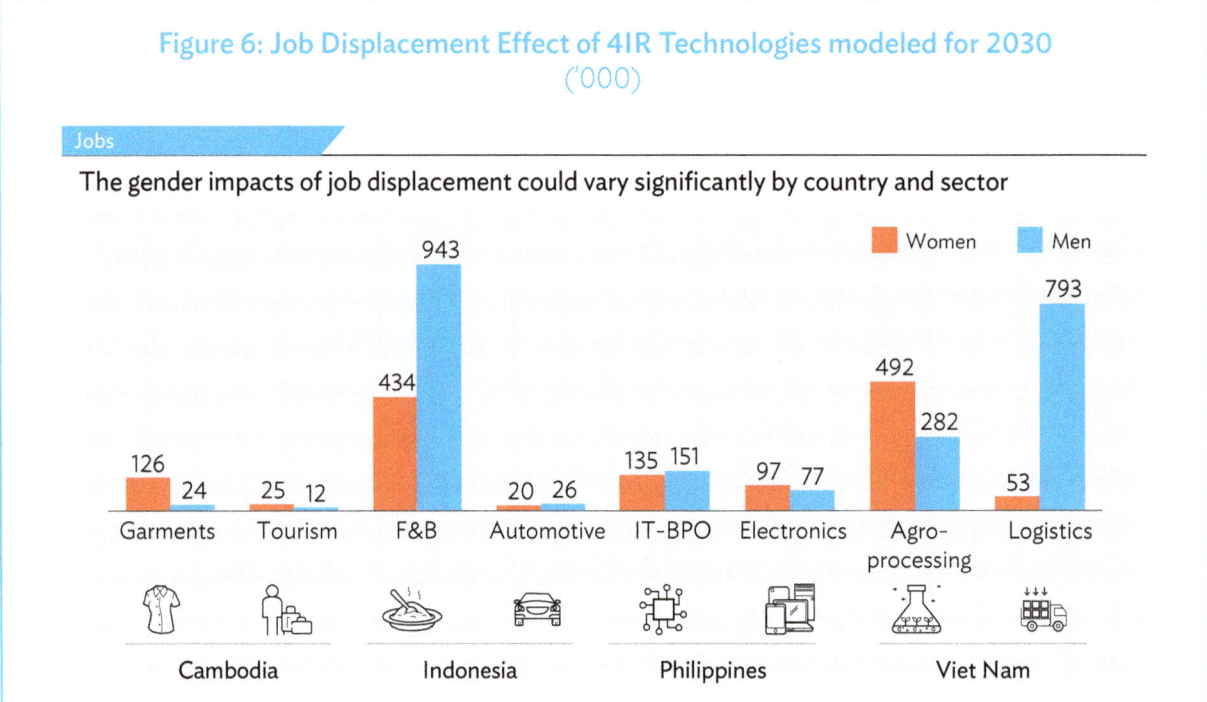

Figure 6: Job Displacement Effect of 4IR Technologies modeled for 2030 ('000)

The gender impacts of job displacement could vary significantly by country and sector

4IR = Industry 4.0 or Fourth Industrial Revolution, F&B = food and beverage, IT-BPO = information technology and business process outsourcing.

Note: Job reductions owing to labor substitution effects of 4IR.

Source: National employment statistics; World Bank STEP survey 2015; RAND Indonesian Family Life Survey; Employer surveys conducted in the four countries (n=393) in 2019; and AlphaBeta modelling.

Job Task Implications

The study examines five types of tasks linked to jobs in each industry and how 4IR could affect them:

(i) **Routine physical.** These tasks involve repetitive and predictable physical work, such as assembling parts on a manufacturing line in a factory.
(ii) **Routine interpersonal.** These tasks involve predictable interactions with other people, such as when a call center worker reads a sales script.
(iii) **Nonroutine physical.** These tasks involve physical work that is not repetitive or predictable, such as when a mechanic diagnoses and repairs a problem in a car engine.
(iv) **Nonroutine interpersonal.** These tasks involve complex or creative interactions with other people, such as supervising coworkers or making speeches or presentations.
(v) **Analytical.** These tasks vary significantly and have strong thinking and analytical components, predominantly working on a computer or other high-tech device.

Research shows that the time spent on analytical tasks is rising. By contrast, the time spent on routine physical tasks could decrease significantly by 2030 (Figure 7). The time spent on nonroutine tasks varies somewhat by industry. This likely reflects that technology will be able to automate routine physical and interpersonal tasks, while humans will focus on more complex tasks that require their problem-solving abilities (Box 3). In IT-BPO, for example, complex tasks could involve call center agents responding to a custom query or a unique problem facing a customer, or IT operators dealing with a security breach.

Figure 7: How Employers Expect 4IR to Affect Time Spent on Tasks by Type from 2018 to 2025

Tasks

Employers believe that 4IR will lead to a shift from routine to non-routine (e.g., tailored customer service) and analytical work

Net percent of survey respondents (%)

	Sector	Analytical	Non-routine inter personal	Non-routine physical	Routine inter personal	Routine physical
Cambodia	Garments	90	60	53	35	(33)
	Tourism	53	56	17	(28)	(21)
Indonesia	F&B	24	3	(26)	(27)	(65)
	Automotive	24	(17)	(41)	(48)	(76)
Philippines	IT-BPO	25	22	15	(35)	(31)
	Electronics	49	10	15	(24)	(48)
Viet Nam	Agro-processing	33	(7)	(20)	(33)	(77)
	Logistics	27	14	(5)	(45)	(74)

( ) = negative, 4IR = Industry 4.0 or Fourth Industrial Revolution, F&B = food and beverage, IT-BPO = information technology and business process outsourcing.

Note: Green indicates more time spent in 2025 than in 2018, and red less time spent.

Source: National employment statistics; World Bank STEP survey 2015; RAND Indonesian Family Life Survey; Employer surveys conducted in the four countries (n=393) in 2019; and AlphaBeta modelling.

Skills Implications

Task shifts could have significant implications for the skills sets each industry requires. The analysis considers 10 categories of skills:[16]

(i) **Critical thinking and adaptive learning.** These skills use logic and reasoning to identify the strengths and weaknesses of alternative solutions, conclusions, or approaches to problems, as well as understanding the implications of new information for both current and future problem-solving and decision-making.

> **Box 3: Estimating Task Shifts**
>
> This analysis uses what the literature calls a "task-based approach." It starts by identifying the employment breakdown of the industry in question using data from labor force surveys. This provides an overview of occupations in the industry and relative employment for 43 occupations aggregated into five major groups: managerial; technical, such as analyst or engineer; administrative, such as secretary; customer facing; and manual, such as floor worker.[a]
>
> A task profile has been developed for each occupation in the industry. Using data collected by the World Bank's Skills Measurement Program, a task profile describes in detail how many hours in an average week the average worker in the occupation spends executing specific tasks. Questions from the survey were used to allocate time spent on task groups. First, the amount of time spent on routine versus nonroutine tasks was determined; then each time allocation was further allocated as physical, interpersonal, or analytical. The result is a profile for each occupation in the industry showing the relative time spent performing tasks in each of the five task groups.
>
> Estimates from employer surveys were used to understand how task profiles would shift with 4IR technology adoption. Employers were asked to estimate the change in aggregate time spent, by task, in their firm—the change in the total time all workers in the firm collectively spend on the task—as a result of 4IR technology adoption over the next 5 years. The fundamental assumption is that the adoption of 4IR technologies changes the task profile of an occupation through the automation of certain tasks, and time in the workday is shifted to other tasks. This generates new task profiles for each occupation in 2030, when 100% of firms are assumed to have adopted 4IR.
>
> [a] Prospera and AlphaBeta. 2019. *Capturing Indonesia's Automation Potential*.
> [b] World Bank. *Skills Measurement Program*.
> Source: Asian Development Bank and AlphaBeta.

(ii) **Written and verbal communication.** This is the ability to read, write, speak, and actively listen.
(iii) **Numeracy.** This is the ability to use mathematics and scientific rules and methods to solve problems.
(iv) **Complex problem-solving.** These skills help identify complex problems and review related information to develop and evaluate options and implement solutions.
(v) **Management.** These skills help allocate financial, material, personnel, and time resources efficiently.
(vi) **Social.** This is the ability to work with people to coordinate, instruct, negotiate, and persuade, featuring service orientation and social perception and empathy.
(vii) **Evaluation, judgment, and decision-making.** These skills are used to understand, monitor, conduct, and improve analysis and sociotechnical systems.
(viii) **Technical.** These are the skills used to design, set up, operate, and maintain technological machines and systems and to correct malfunctions in their application.
(ix) **Computer literacy.** These skills allow workers to use computers and digital applications in their jobs, effectively using email, word processing, internet searches, and data entry.
(x) **Digital/ICT.** These skills allow workers to pursue inherently digital occupations and perform complex tasks in a digital environment, as well as maintaining digital infrastructure such as advanced spreadsheets, financial software, graphic design, statistical analysis, software programming, or computer networks.

> ### Box 4: Estimating Skills Changes
>
> Computation of current skills profiles for each occupation in an industry used data from the World Bank's Skills Measurement Program questionnaire Module 6: Work Skills. Based on survey responses, a value on a scale of 0–3 was assigned to skills, with 0 for an unused skill and 3 for highly advanced skill needed. The score measures both importance and the skill competence required for each skill category.
>
> Future skills profiles used two data sources: (i) data on skill and education requirements from job profiles for occupations, obtained from online job portals; and (ii) information about changes in skill requirements from employer surveys.
>
> The collected job postings were analyzed in detail and assigned an importance and skill competency score for each of the 10 skill categories. The postings were also categorized into the five job groups identified above: managerial, administrative, technical, customer facing, and manual.
>
> As a parallel second estimate, survey data from employers were leveraged to understand which skill categories would gain in importance with the adoption of 4IR technology. Based on employers' responses, percentage changes in importance were calculated for each of the five job groups. Applying these scores to the current skills profiles based on the Skills Measurement Program yielded a second set of estimates for future skills profiles.
>
> The future skills profiles used to estimate the skills gap were then computed as an average of the two estimates, and the skills gap by occupation was measured as the difference in importance scores between current and future skill profiles.
>
> Source: Asian Development Bank and AlphaBeta.

The analysis highlights some significant changes in skill requirements in each industry (Figure 8). Interestingly, "evaluation, judgment, and decision-making" is predicted to become the most important skill in all industries except tourism, where it will be "written and verbal communication," and electronics, where it will be "numeracy." Management skills are generally seen to become less important relative to other skills as 4IR technologies perhaps make it simpler to monitor workers.

Skills Supply Trends

Figure 9 breaks down additional demand for training workers will require in each industry under 4IR technology adoption. This reflects the volume of training needed to lift today's workforce from the skills required in 2018 to the skill competence required by 2030, considering only changes brought by the adoption of 4IR technologies. All eight industries together will require 169 million additional person-trainings by 2030.[17] Most of the training requirements will likely be met by on-the-job training,[18] with the rest split evenly between short-term professional training[19] and longer-term formal training.[20]

---

[17] One person-training trains one worker in one skill from the average level required by his or her occupation in his or her industry in 2018 to the level required in 2030.
[18] On-the-job training refers to training conducting day to day, such as senior staff instructing junior staff or running internal seminars.
[19] Short-term professional training refers to short (between 1 day and 5 months) courses conducted by professional internal or external instructors (e.g., weekend seminars, boot camps).
[20] Longer formal trainings refer to trainings longer than 6 months for which workers would likely have to take time off from their jobs. This includes returning to formal education, such as to obtain a degree.

Figure 8: Relative Importance of Occupational Skills in 2030

Skills

Changes in the importance of different skills will vary by industry and country

- 🟩 Skills of increasing relative importance from 2018–2030
- 🟧 Skills with decreasing relative importance from 2018–2030
- ⬜ Skills with no change in relative importance

	Cambodia		Indonesia		Philippines		Viet Nam	
Skills	Garments	Tourism	F&B	Automotive	IT-BPO	Electronics	Agro-processing	Logistics
Critical thinking and adaptive learning	4	6	2	3	6	8	8	5
Written and verbal communication	5	1	3	4	3	5	5	4
Numeracy	3	4	4	7	2	1	2	3
Complex problem solving	8	9	6	8	7	7	7	7
Management	2	5	5	6	8	6	6	6
Social	6	3	8	2	4	9	4	2
Evaluation, judgment, and decision-making	1	2	1	1	1	2	1	1
Technical	7	8	7	9	9	3	3	8
Computer literacy	9	7	9	5	5	4	9	9
Digital/ICT skills	10	10	10	10	10	10	10	10

F&B = food and beverage, ICT = information and communication technology, IT-BPO = information technology and business process outsourcing.

Note: Ranking of 1–10, where 1 is the most important skill in 2030.

Source: National employment statistics; World Bank STEP survey 2015; RAND Indonesian Family Life Survey; Employer surveys conducted in the four countries (n=393) in 2019; and AlphaBeta modelling.

Figure 9: Additional Training Required by 2030 by Industry and Training Channel

Training

Much of the incremental skills demand will need to be met by "on-the-job" training

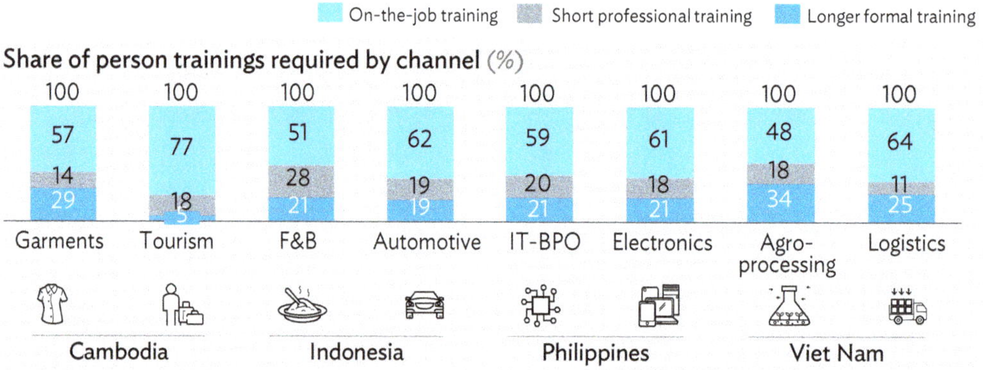

- On-the-job training
- Short professional training
- Longer formal training

Share of person trainings required by channel (%)

	Garments	Tourism	F&B	Automotive	IT-BPO	Electronics	Agro-processing	Logistics
On-the-job training	57	77	51	62	59	61	48	64
Short professional training	14	18	28	19	20	18	18	11
Longer formal training	29	5	21	19	21	21	34	25
Total	100	100	100	100	100	100	100	100

Cambodia: Garments, Tourism | Indonesia: F&B, Automotive | Philippines: IT-BPO, Electronics | Viet Nam: Agro-processing, Logistics

F&B = food and beverage, IT-BPO = information technology and business process outsourcing.

Note: Figures include rounding adjustments.

Source: National employment statistics; World Bank STEP survey 2015; RAND Indonesian Family Life Survey; Employer surveys conducted in the four countries (n=393) in 2019; and AlphaBeta modelling.

Box 5: Estimating Training Requirements

Training requirements can be quantified as person-trainings, one of which trains one worker in one skill in the competence required in his or her industry in 2018 to the competence required in 2030 under 4IR technology adoption. Hence, training one worker who is competent in 2018 to the competence required in 2030 would require one person-training for each skill that needs improvement.

Understanding the type and length of training needed requires consideration of two factors: (i) the degree of skill improvement required and (ii) different workers' access to different training channels.

An individual's training needs will depend on whether he or she requires skill improvement from basic to intermediate, intermediate to advanced, or basic to advanced. For example, a worker who requires only basic technical skills today but advanced technical skills in 2030 under 4IR technology adoption will likely require more training than another worker who has to improve his or her skills only from intermediate to advanced. The same goes for workers who do not need a particular skill today but will require it in 2030, either basic, intermediate, or advanced.

The length of training required to obtain a certain skill level apart, access to training may not be the same for all workers in an industry. For example, workers who are laid off and therefore not able to receive on-the-job training will require formal training before being able to find a new job. Similarly, for future generations of workers, such as students currently in formal education or training, it may make more sense to embed skills training in their curriculum rather than waiting to train them on the job. Skill demand analysis identified three categories of workers affected by 4IR:

Workers who need new skills. These workers will likely lose their current jobs to automation, so they will need training to become employable in newly created jobs.

Workers who need their skills enhanced. These workers will likely remain in their occupations but the adoption of 4IR technologies will demand new skills and upgrades to existing skills to meet their occupation's future skills profile.

Future workers. These additional workers will be required to fill jobs generated by growing demand. Not having previously worked in the industry, they can join as either new graduates or professional hires from other industries.

Distinctions between types of workers are important because the different types have access to different training channels. While future workers, for example, are likely to receive some of their skills training in formal education, returning to formal education is unlikely to be an option for workers who need new skills and will continue to be employed during their training.

Source: Asian Development Bank and AlphaBeta.

CHAPTER 2
Overview of the Training Landscape

This chapter provides insights into the performance of technical and vocational education and training (TVET) in each country as they prepare for the challenges that will arise as a result of Industry 4.0 (4IR) technology adoption. The insights are drawn from surveys of training institutions in Cambodia, Indonesia, the Philippines, and Viet Nam, complemented by the employer surveys discussed in Chapter 1.

Encouragingly, alignment is generally strong between the skills that training institutions believe will be particularly important under 4IR and the perceptions of employers. However, some training institutions may struggle to keep pace with the rate of change in the demand for skills. Almost half of the training institutions surveyed review and update their curricula less than annually, for example, and only about half provide information on job market conditions to their students.

There seems to be severe misalignment between training institutions' assessments of how well prepared their graduates are for work and employers' expectations with regard to graduates' command of the skills required to perform well in entry-level jobs, as well as of general and job-specific skills. The widest gap is in Cambodia: 59% of training institutions in Cambodia believe graduates are well prepared for entry-level positions whereas only 11% of employers in the garment and tourism industries agree.

Over half of training institutions reported that they already operated programs dedicated to 4IR skills, and an even higher share in all four countries reported plans to develop or expand programs for 4IR by 2025. While this is an encouraging trend, it is critical to assess the quality of such training and its alignment with employer needs. A structured assessment of training needs for 4IR is required, as 63%–90% of training institutions surveyed across the four countries stated that they needed additional financial and technical support for 4IR skills development.

Industry 4.0 Readiness

To better understand the supply of talent and skills for the adoption of 4IR, surveys were commissioned to cover 236 training institutions in Cambodia, Indonesia, the Philippines, and Viet Nam. The surveys primarily covered TVET institutions, most of them private, from the secondary to the tertiary level, as well as those providing midcareer training. Institutions of different sizes were sampled, the smallest training fewer than 100 students annually and the largest training over 100,000. Most institutions surveyed train 200 to 1,000 students annually.

While most institutions describe themselves as well prepared for 4IR, many nevertheless request additional technical and financial support (Figure 10). Indonesian training institutions were the most likely to report that they felt prepared for 4IR; the reported readiness of Cambodian and Vietnamese training institutions was generally lower. Even in Indonesia, however, 90% of institutions felt they would need additional technical and financial support to fully prepare for 4IR.

Figure 10: Training Institution Perceptions of Their Readiness for 4IR

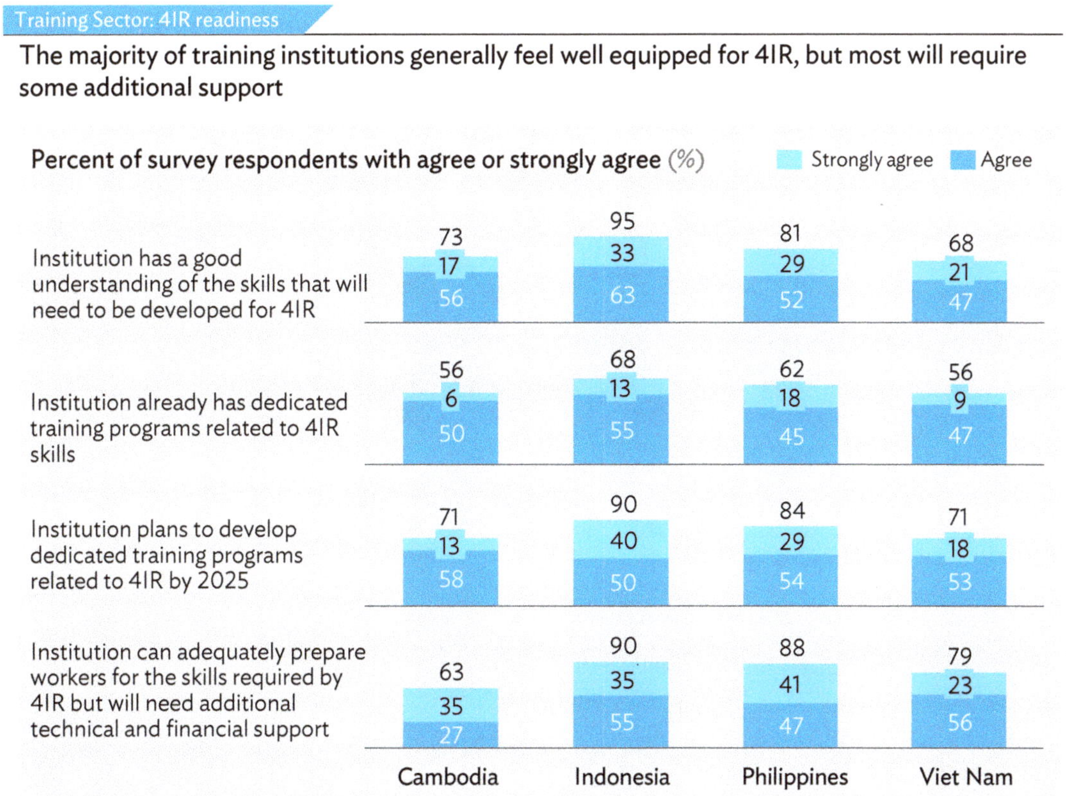

Training Sector: 4IR readiness

The majority of training institutions generally feel well equipped for 4IR, but most will require some additional support

Percent of survey respondents with agree or strongly agree (%) — Strongly agree | Agree

Statement	Cambodia	Indonesia	Philippines	Viet Nam
Institution has a good understanding of the skills that will need to be developed for 4IR	73 (17 / 56)	95 (33 / 63)	81 (29 / 52)	68 (21 / 47)
Institution already has dedicated training programs related to 4IR skills	56 (6 / 50)	68 (13 / 55)	62 (18 / 45)	56 (9 / 47)
Institution plans to develop dedicated training programs related to 4IR by 2025	71 (13 / 58)	90 (40 / 50)	84 (29 / 54)	71 (18 / 53)
Institution can adequately prepare workers for the skills required by 4IR but will need additional technical and financial support	63 (35 / 27)	90 (35 / 55)	88 (41 / 47)	79 (23 / 56)

4IR = Industry 4.0 or Fourth Industrial Revolution.

Source: Training institution surveys in Cambodia, Indonesia, the Philippines, and Viet Nam. n=239. The surveys were conducted in 2019.

Alignment is generally strong between the skills that training institutions believe will be particularly important under 4IR and the perceptions of employers. In the Philippines, for example, the skill category most training institutions deem will become much more important over the next 5 years of 4IR adoption is "technical," closely followed by "digital/ICT," "complex problem-solving," and "computer literacy." The employer ranking is similar.

Curricula

Aligning curricula with actual industry needs is one of the most important aspects of an effective training and education sector—but often also the biggest challenge. It relies on frequent updating and close communication with industry, given the speed of change in 4IR technologies in the workplace. Regular curriculum reviews are therefore critical to keep pace with skill changes. However, up to half of surveyed training institutions review and update their curricula less often than annually (Figure 11).

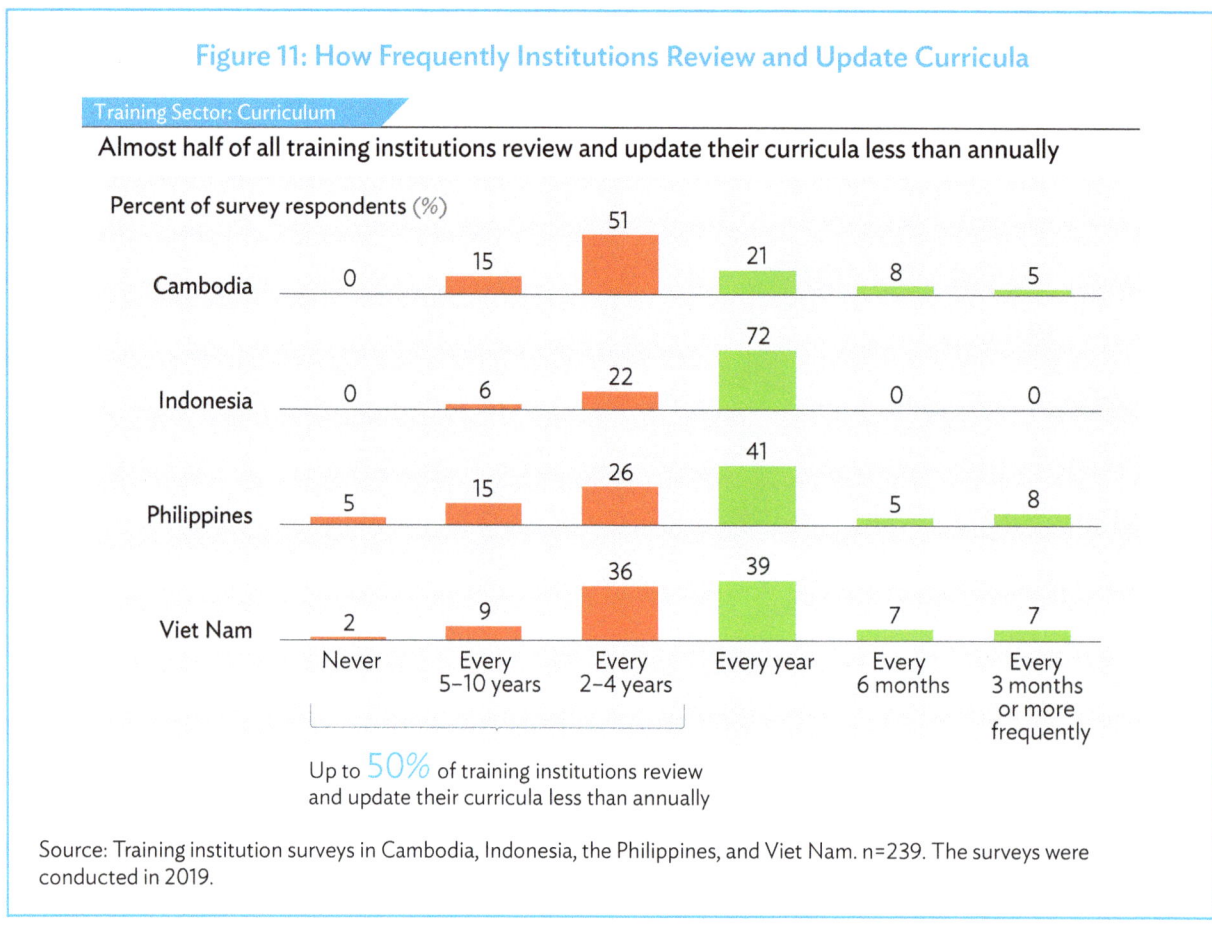

Figure 11: How Frequently Institutions Review and Update Curricula

Source: Training institution surveys in Cambodia, Indonesia, the Philippines, and Viet Nam. n=239. The surveys were conducted in 2019.

Another aspect to consider is curriculum content. According to vocational students in Indonesia, on-the-job training and hands-on learning are two of the three most effective instructional modes.[21] Denmark, Finland, France, Germany, Norway, and Switzerland, for example, spend 50%–75% of instruction time in upper-secondary school on practical or on-site training.[22] Training institution survey results are somewhat mixed in this regard. Training institutions in Cambodia, the Philippines, and Indonesia reported high shares of training time in workplace activities; the share is significantly lower in Viet Nam (Figure 12).

While about half of the surveyed training institutions reported providing courses that were relevant for 4IR, the record is mixed with regard to their adoption of 4IR technologies in the classroom to facilitate training delivery (Figure 13). Most training institutions offer online training modules but fewer adopt other technologies such as virtual reality and simulators. As the latter technologies are more nascent and expensive, their limited uptake likely reflects financial constraints and a lack of information about the latest applications. Interestingly, despite Cambodian businesses' low understanding of 4IR, as Chapter 1 showed, Cambodian training institutes reported a relatively high share of 4IR technology use in their teaching.

---

[21] Asia Philanthropy Circle. 2017. *Catalysing Productive Livelihood: A Guide to Education Interventions with an Accelerated Path to Scale and Impact.*
[22] M. Kuczera. 2010. *Learning for Jobs—The OECD International Survey of VET Systems: First Results and Technical Report.* Paris: OECD.

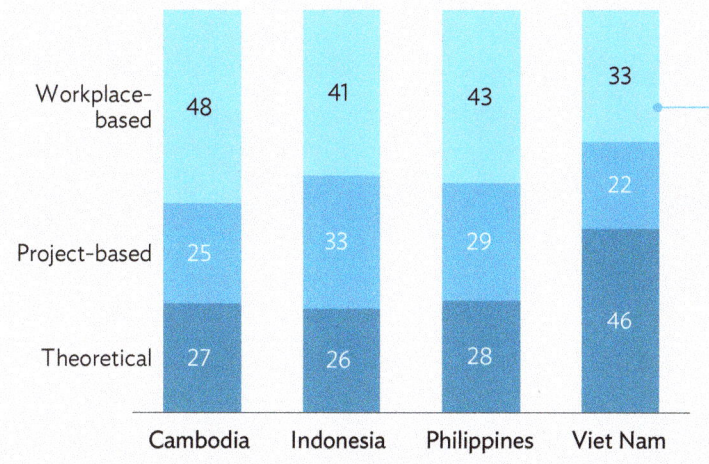

Figure 12: Share of Learning Time by Type of Training

Training Sector: Curriculum

There is a lower focus on workplace or practical training than is seen in leading international vocational programs

Average percentage share of total time spent on training type at surveyed institutions (%)

	Cambodia	Indonesia	Philippines	Viet Nam
Workplace-based	48	41	43	33
Project-based	25	33	29	22
Theoretical	27	26	28	46

According to OECD research, more than three-quarters of vocational training programs in Denmark, Germany, Finland, France, Norway, and Switzerland at the upper-secondary level spend 50%–75% of instructional time in practical or onsite training.

OECD = Organisation for Economic Co-operation and Development.

Note: "Theoretical" refers to lectures, "project-based" refers to student projects, and "workplace-based" refers to on-the-job training such as industry apprenticeships.

Source: Training institution surveys in Cambodia, Indonesia, the Philippines, and Viet Nam. n=239. The surveys were conducted in 2019.

Many training institutions offer, in addition to training courses, a range of programs and activities that aim to provide students with better information on career opportunities and access to support (Figure 14). While most training institutions provide career advice to students, fewer provide information on job market conditions, such as wages and job prospects, in different industries.

Industry Engagement

The surveyed training institutions have very strong interaction with potential employers. Most of them in all four countries reported that they communicated and coordinated with employers at least several times per year (Figure 15).

Except in Cambodia, training institutes commonly conduct industry apprenticeships as part of their engagement with employers (Figure 16). Far fewer offer teaching placements for industry professionals, except in Indonesia.

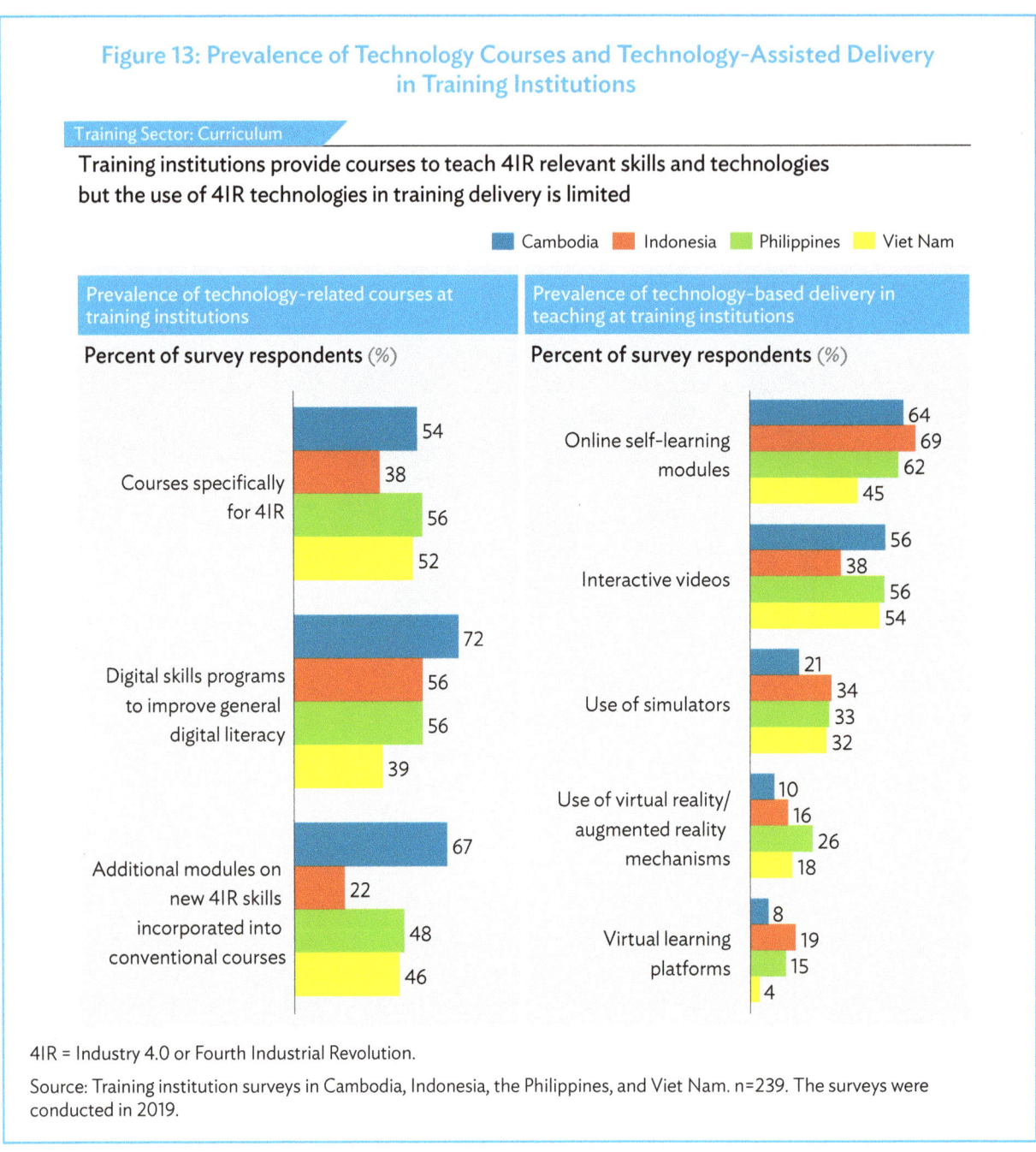

Figure 13: Prevalence of Technology Courses and Technology-Assisted Delivery in Training Institutions

4IR = Industry 4.0 or Fourth Industrial Revolution.
Source: Training institution surveys in Cambodia, Indonesia, the Philippines, and Viet Nam. n=239. The surveys were conducted in 2019.

While training institutions appear to engage employers actively, active engagement by employers seems to be more limited. In the Philippines, for example, only half of training institutions receive train-the-teacher support from industry, only 38% are able to use employer-provided equipment and facilities for hands-on training, and under 23% offer teaching placements for industry professionals. In Cambodia, just 3% of institutions offer such teaching placements.

Figure 14: Programs Provided in Addition to Training Courses

Training Sector: Curriculum

In addition to training courses, a number of training institutions provide programs such as career advice, scholarships, and company visits

Percent of survey respondents (%)

	Cambodia	Indonesia	Philippines	Viet Nam
Meetings with professional career coaches for career advice	79	78	56	79
Scholarships for students from low-income backgrounds	77	38	67	70
Visits to companies	72	63	49	63
Preparation of CVs or resumes	79	53	74	52
Information on employment type/wages of alumni	54	63	62	52
Visits from company representatives	82	47	41	52
Information about wages and job prospects in different fields	56	56	48	45
Information on graduation/program completion rates	54	56	62	45
Job application and interview support	62	38	80	43
Meetings with counsellors for non-career advice (e.g., financial, personal)	46	28	38	39

CV = curriculum vitae.

Source: Training institution surveys in Cambodia, Indonesia, the Philippines, and Viet Nam. n=239. The surveys were conducted in 2019.

Figure 15: Frequency of Training Institution Communication with Employers

Training Sector: Employers

Most training institutions report that they engage regularly with employers in their relevant sectors

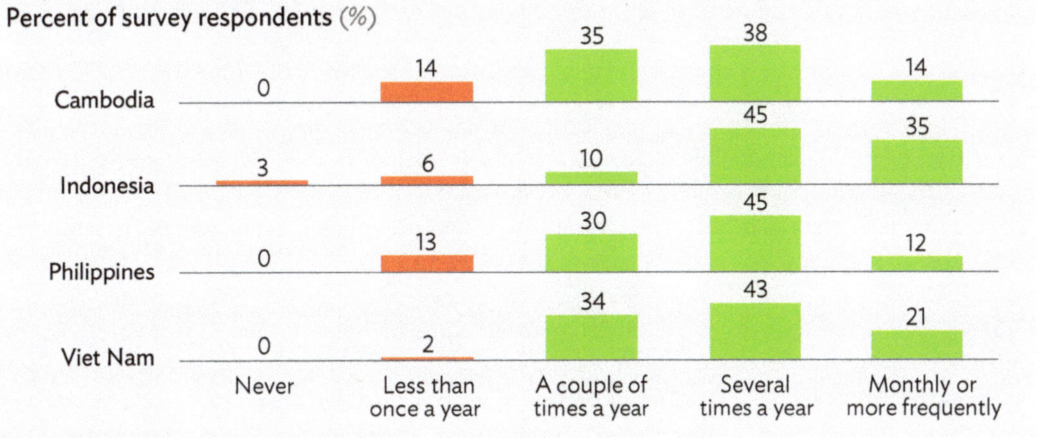

Percent of survey respondents (%)

	Never	Less than once a year	A couple of times a year	Several times a year	Monthly or more frequently
Cambodia	0	14	35	38	14
Indonesia	3	6	10	45	35
Philippines	0	13	30	45	12
Viet Nam	0	2	34	43	21

Source: Training institution surveys in Cambodia, Indonesia, the Philippines, and Viet Nam. n=239. The surveys were conducted in 2019.

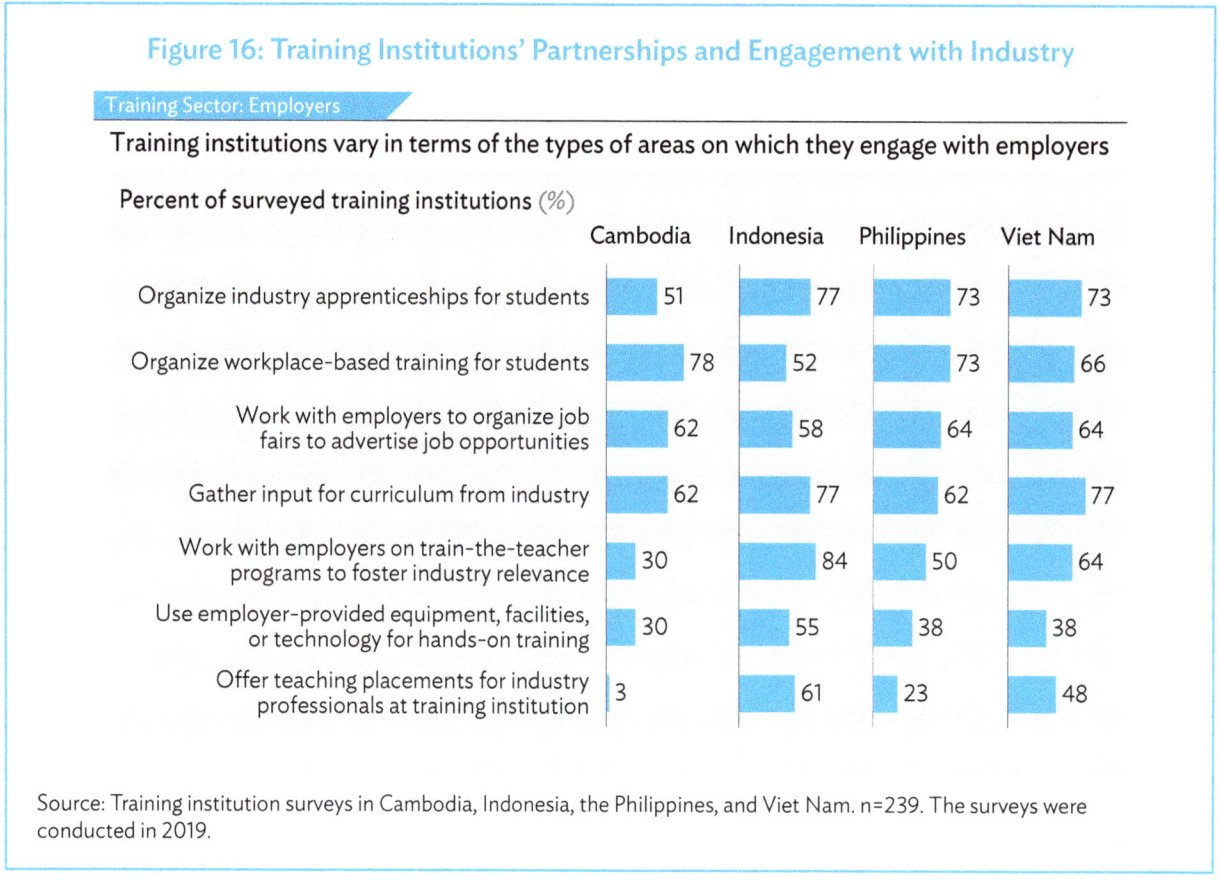

Teachers, Trainers, and Instructors

It is encouraging that many training institutions actively assess the performance and professional development of their teaching and training staff, with the vast majority of institutions providing frequent feedback and giving formal annual or semiannual performance reviews (Figure 17). However, only the Philippines seems to place as much emphasis on staff professional development.

Performance and Policy Support

Most training institutions in the Philippines and Viet Nam have trouble filling student spots in their courses; this seems to be less of a problem in Cambodia and Indonesia (Figure 18). These difficulties appear to stem largely from a lack of competitive pricing, potential trainees' inability to differentiate programs, and trainees' lack of knowledge of the programs.

Training institutions look to governments to address some of these challenges (Figure 19). For example, most training institutions believe they could benefit greatly from government inspection and certification to assess institution quality. This finding appears consistent with earlier survey results in which training institutions reported that students lacked information on the quality of different training providers.

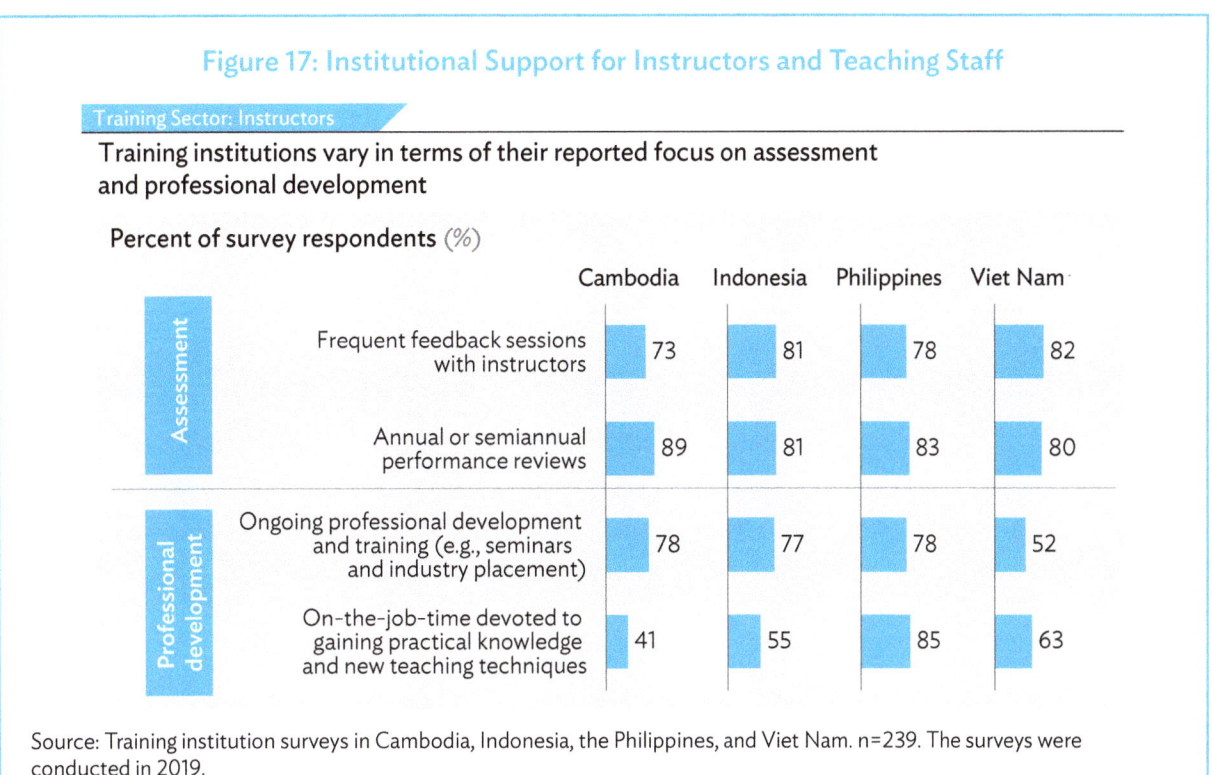

Figure 17: Institutional Support for Instructors and Teaching Staff

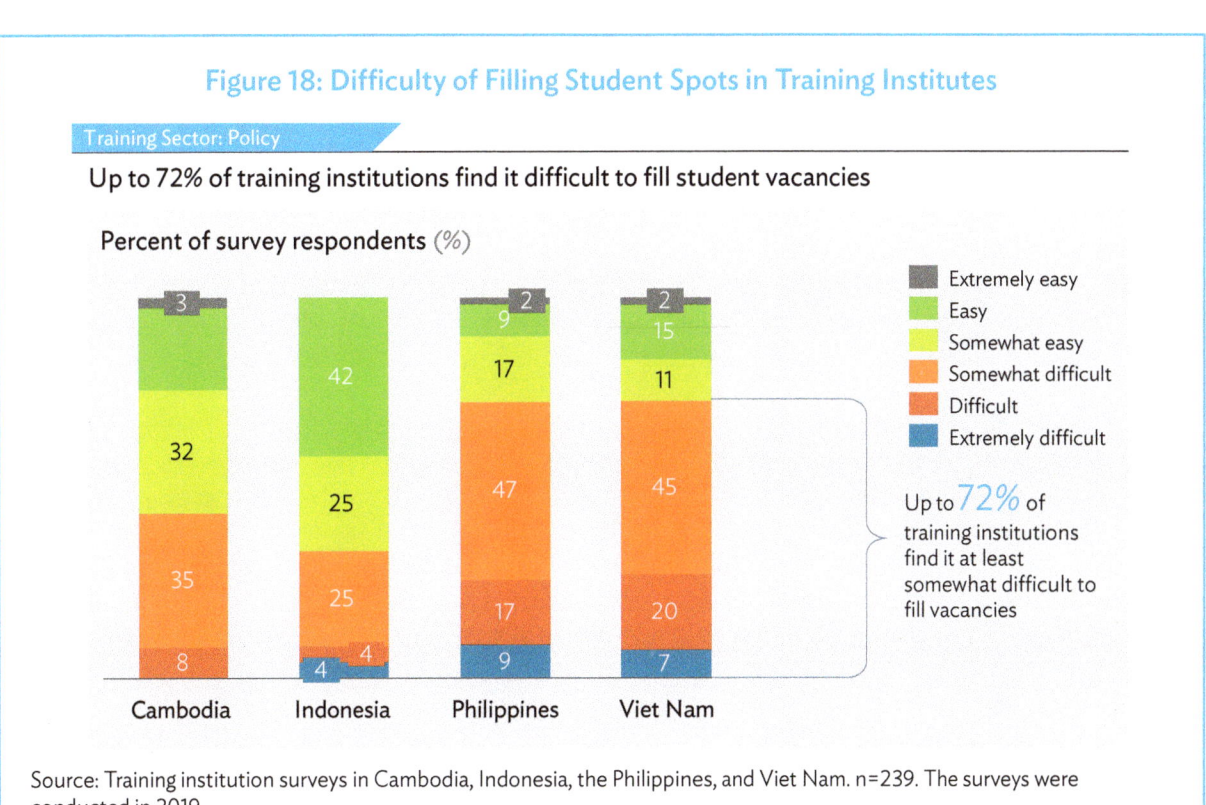

Figure 18: Difficulty of Filling Student Spots in Training Institutes

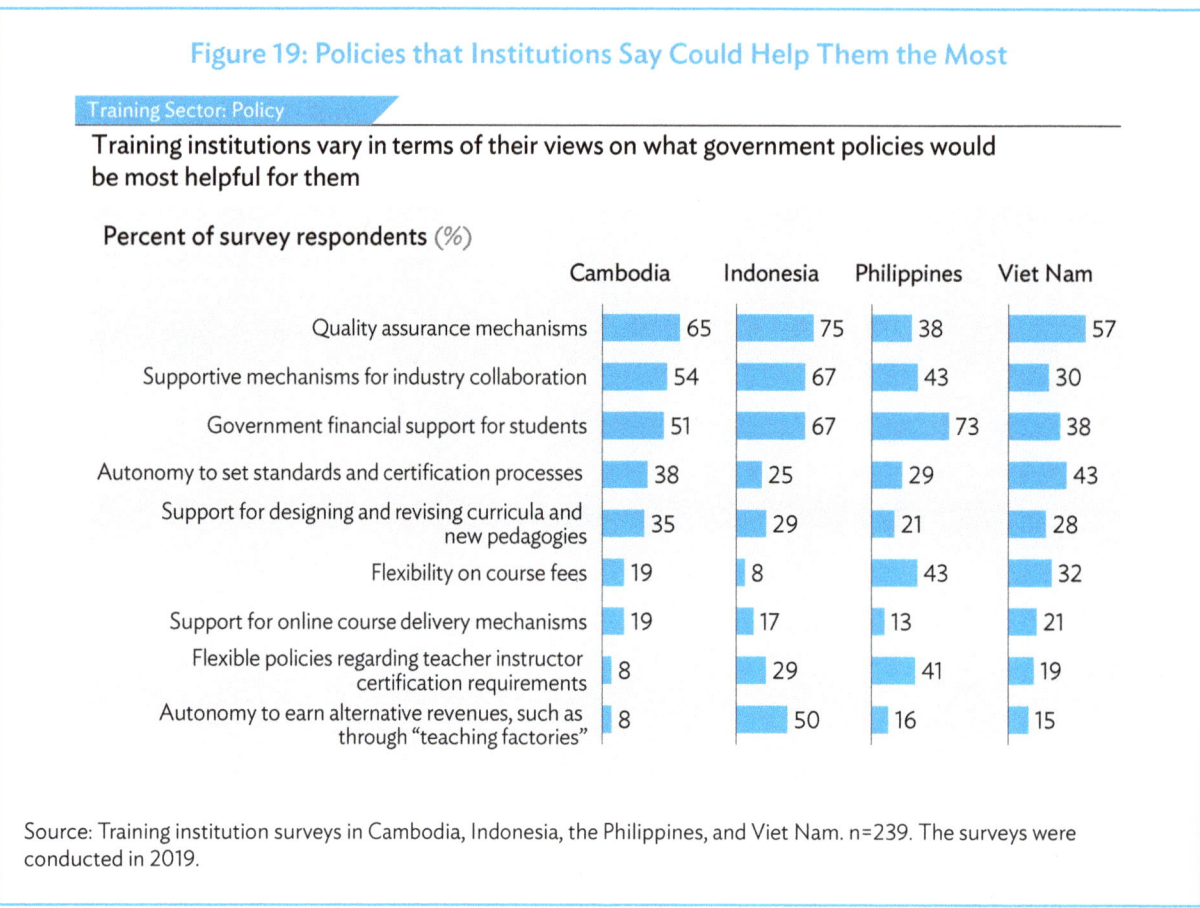

Figure 19: Policies that Institutions Say Could Help Them the Most

Source: Training institution surveys in Cambodia, Indonesia, the Philippines, and Viet Nam. n=239. The surveys were conducted in 2019.

Supply and Demand Mismatches

According to the training institutions surveyed, the most common reason that graduates may not be able to find jobs is that employers do not recognize their certifications (Figure 20). An exception is Cambodia, where a lack of job opportunities was reported as the biggest challenge.

Another mismatch between industry and training institutions relates to their respective assessments of the skills and competence of graduates—either basic, intermediate, or advanced—when they finish their training or education. Training institutions believe that graduates are prepared to work, but employers require greater competence to perform well in entry-level positions, as well as higher general and job-specific skills (Figure 21). Perception gaps are widest in Cambodia and Indonesia. While 59% of training institutions in Cambodia believe their graduates are well prepared for entry-level positions, only 11% of employers in garments and tourism agree. Similarly, in Indonesia, while 96% of training institutions believe their graduates are well prepared for entry-level positions, only 32% of employers agree.

This significant mismatch in skills expectations between employers and training institutions is particularly surprising given that training institutions reported frequent engagement with employers. These results suggest that, while training institutions may understand which skill categories are rising in importance for 4IR, their implementation of skills training does not match industry requirements.

Figure 20: Reasons Students Cannot Find Jobs after Graduation, by Prevalence

Training Sector: Students

Training institutions believe a lack of certification recognition and of preparation for jobs by training programs are key employment barriers

Ranking score: 1 –Most common; 5 –Least common   ■ Biggest barrier cited

	Cambodia	Indonesia	Philippines	Viet Nam
Graduates' certifications are not well-recognized by employers	2.9	**1.8**	2.5	**2.2**
Education and training programs do not adequately prepare job seekers for job opportunities	3.1	2.7	2.9	2.8
Not enough job opportunities	**2.0**	3.9	3.0	3.1
Not enough opportunities for job seekers to complete relevant education or training for job opportunities	3.6	3.4	3.3	3.5
Enough jobs but students unaware of job opportunities	3.6	3.2	3.3	3.4

Source: Training institution surveys in Cambodia, Indonesia, the Philippines, and Viet Nam. n=239. The surveys were conducted in 2019.

Figure 21: Perceptions of How Well Graduates Are Prepared for Entry-Level Positions

Training Sector: Students

On average, training institutions are much more optimistic about the preparedness of graduates for work than what employers report

Percent of survey respondents who agree or strongly agree with the following statements (%)

	Cambodia		Indonesia		Philippines		Viet Nam	
	Training institutions	Employers	Training institutions	Employers	Training institutions	Employers	Training institutions	Employers
Graduates are adequately prepared for entry-level positions	59	11	96	32	90	55	80	38
Graduates have the appropriate "general" skills	78	8	92	39	90	57	80	53
Graduates have the appropriate "job-specific" skills	65	13	92	31	88	59	78	59

Note: In each country, the employer response represents an average of responses from employers surveyed in the two sectors surveyed (equally weighted across sectors).

Source: Training institution surveys in Cambodia, Indonesia, the Philippines, and Viet Nam. n=239. The surveys were conducted in 2019.

CHAPTER 3
National Policy Responses

A thorough review of all current policies and programs pursued by governments, industry, and civil society in Cambodia, Indonesia, the Philippines, and Viet Nam reveals a range of strategies that seek to ready national workforces for Industry 4.0 (4IR). Despite efforts in many countries to foster collaboration between governments, industry, and civil society to create retraining frameworks for workers, some common gaps remain. Incentives are weak for employers and workers to participate in skills development, curricula and skills certification mechanisms are rigid, and social protection mechanisms for flexible workers are lacking. In terms of implementation, common gaps persist in terms of a lack of 4IR vision that is shared and coordinated across ministries and levels of government.

Review of Industry 4.0 Policy Actions in Each of the Four Countries

Policy assessment draws on government documents on 4IR and skills policy, academic literature, reviews of government policies, and newly conducted surveys in the four countries.

Country policies and programs are grouped into nine action areas assessed as crucial to managing the impact of 4IR on jobs and skills.[23] Figure 22 shows the current degree of focus on each action area by country, rated *strong*, *moderate*, or *weak* compared with international best practice.

The focus on aspects of the 4IR skills agenda varies significantly by country, but some areas generally enjoy greater attention: (i) fostering collaboration between governments, industry, and civil society to create training frameworks for 4IR and (ii) stimulating greater 4IR technology adoption across firms and workers. Scope exists for much greater focus on (i) building awareness of jobs and skills in demand under 4IR, (ii) strengthening incentives for employers and workers to participate in skills development, (iii) ensuring the relevance and agility of education and training curriculums, (iv) encouraging a focus on skills rather than just educational qualifications, (v) building inclusive models that allow underserved groups to benefit from 4IR, (vi) creating social protection mechanisms for flexible workers in the gig economy, and (vii) establishing effective lifelong learning models.

Stimulate Industry 4.0 Adoption and Worker Reskilling Efforts
Ensure strong and even adoption of 4IR across firms and workers. A policy framework that seeks to harness the benefits of 4IR for the economy includes actions that create an enabling environment for firms to adopt technology. A global 4IR readiness assessment in 2018 indicated that all four countries

---

[23] Based on AlphaBeta research on international best practices for policy actions that manage the impact of Industry 4.0 on jobs and skills. For details of these best practices, see Microsoft and AlphaBeta. 2019. *Preparing for AI: The Implications of Artificial Intelligence for Jobs and Skills in Asian Economies.*

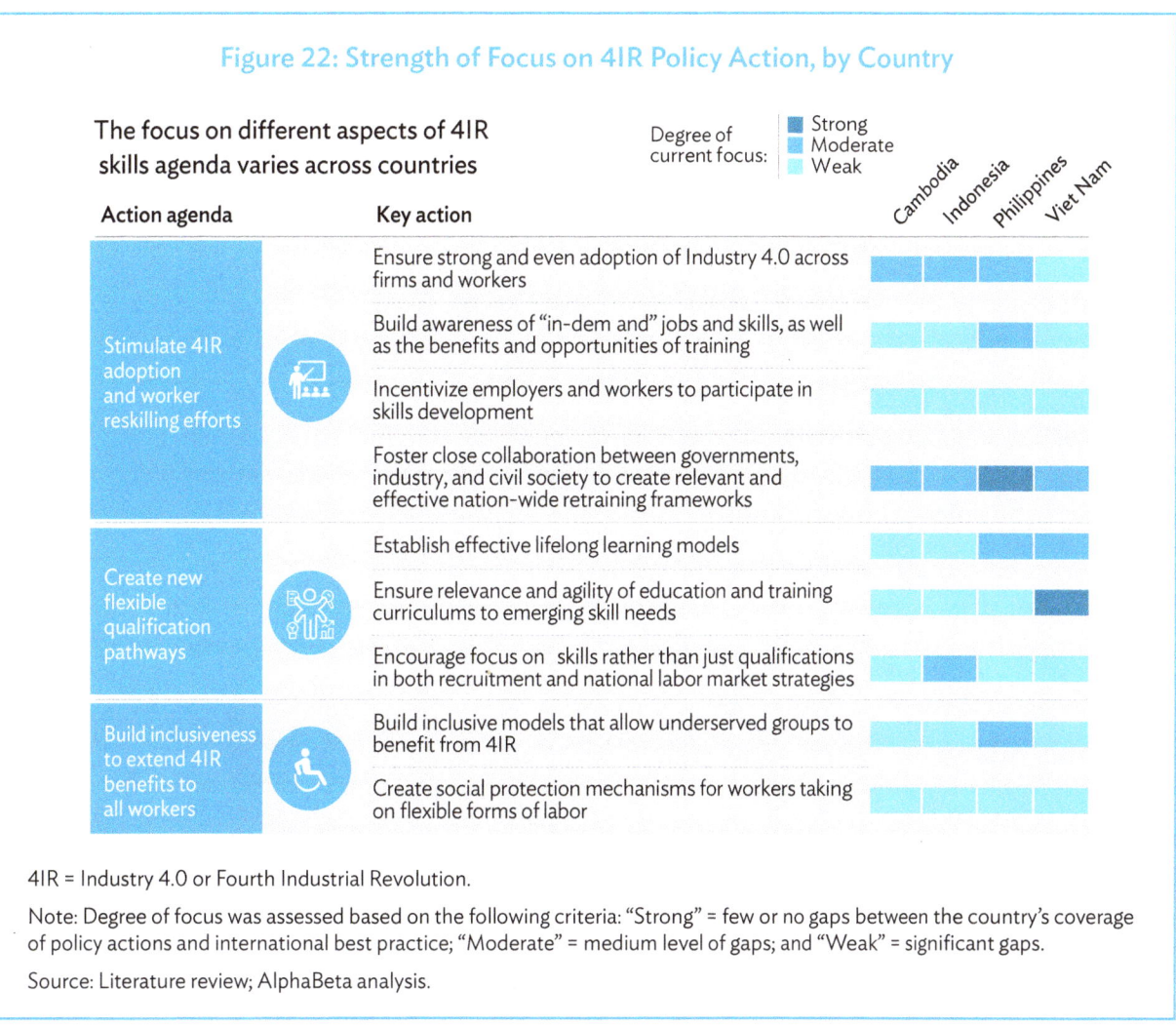

had major gaps to close to fully ready themselves for 4IR. While the Philippines was assessed to be in the early planning phase for 4IR, Cambodia, Indonesia, and Viet Nam were considered only nascent in 4IR development. This was because of their relatively weak performance in a number of areas, notably robust institutional frameworks, investment in human capital, and technology adoption.[24]

While Cambodia, Indonesia, and the Philippines demonstrated *moderate* focus in this action area, Viet Nam's focus was assessed as *weak* (Figure 22). Common policy priorities with *moderate* focus were the expansion of digital infrastructure to broaden access to digital technologies and the facilitation of foreign technology transfer in Cambodia and Indonesia, and the provision of financial and technical support to catalyze technology adoption for micro, small, and medium-sized enterprises in Cambodia and the Philippines. Conversely, while broad policy aspirations to facilitate technology adoption, such as incentivizing research and development (R&D) investment, were highlighted in Viet Nam's forthcoming National Strategy for 4IR, they have yet to be implemented.[25]

---

[24] World Economic Forum (WEF) and A. T. Kearney. 2018. *Readiness for the Future of Production Report 2018*.
[25] Draft National Strategy for 4IR. Unpublished. Obtained August 2019.

Several policy actions in the three countries with *moderate* focus stand out as particularly strong models that could be considered by the other countries. These include the Philippines' regional Centers of Excellence program, under which 17 training institutions, evenly distributed geographically throughout the country, have been selected for upgrading to train Filipinos in the skills required for the future economy.[26] Another positive example is the Indonesia 4.0 Readiness Index developed by the Ministry of Industry, whose detailed assessment of 4IR readiness in five priority sectors has been used to guide specific 4IR technology adoption strategies for firms in each sector.[27]

Assessed against international best practice, however, all four countries have further scope for greater investment in domestic R&D talent and projects, fostering industry–research partnerships, and tackling technology costs and other adoption barriers for MSMEs (footnote 23).

Build awareness of jobs and skills in demand, as well as the benefits and opportunities of training.
It is important that governments, workers, and employers alike be informed of emerging skills needs under 4IR, potential skills gaps, and opportunities for training in those skills. A recent survey of the attitudes of employers and their workers toward acquiring new skills, or "reskilling," for AI in three of the four focus countries—Indonesia, the Philippines, and Viet Nam—found many employers were unaware of suitable training programs for their workers, and almost half of workers in some countries stated that they did not know what courses to take.[28] Both findings point to a lack of understanding of reskilling opportunities despite government efforts to catalyze them.

The focus on this action area is *moderate* in the Philippines but *weak* in the other three countries (Figure 22). The Government of the Philippines has devoted considerable attention to establishing a regularly updated database of jobs and skills in demand, and industry bodies increasingly focus on identifying 4IR skills needs. In the other three countries, priorities still center largely on a generic mapping of skills demanded by industry, with little focus on the specific skills needed under 4IR. Where this focus exists, as in the development of a 4IR-relevant course of the Ministry of Industry of Indonesia, nascent and small-scale initiatives have yet to be implemented nationwide.[29]

A particularly strong approach that other focus countries could consider is the Philippines' nationwide mapping of 21st century skills. Undertaken by the Department of Labor Employment, this study assessed over 100,000 Filipinos on their competence across 15 defined skills using in-depth consultations with employers across a range of industries, to map emerging 4IR skills needs and gaps observed in the workforce.[30]

Assessed against international best practice, however, all four countries could give greater attention to mapping the skills required for 4IR, projected skills gaps based on the current workforce, and the specific training programs needed to address them (footnote 23).

---

[26] Based on consultations with the Technical Education and Skills Development Authority (TESDA) and ADB in July 2019.
[27] Readiness was assessed along five dimensions: organizational culture (the willingness of leadership to invest in 4IR), skills and human capital, operations, products and services, and the degree of technology adoption. Source: Consultation with the Ministry of Industry in July 2019.
[28] Microsoft and International Data Corporation. 2018. *Digital Transformation to Contribute US$8 billion to the Philippines GDP by 2021.*
[29] Based on consultation with the Ministry of Industry in July 2019.
[30] Philippine Talent Map.

Incentivize employers and workers to participate in skills development. This focus is assessed as *weak* across all four countries (Figure 22). It is, however, an important area for policy action, particularly as cost is one of the largest barriers to skills development. Studies, surveys, and stakeholder consultations reflect low rates of worker training undertaken by employers in the four countries. Fewer than a quarter of Indonesian companies, for example, conduct formal in-house training for their workers.[31] In the Philippines, a recent survey by the World Economic Forum found 4% more employers would prefer to hire new permanent staff than retrain existing workers to attain the required skills.[32] Stakeholder consultations in Cambodia and Viet Nam similarly reflected limited investment by firms in worker training.

While these countries have set out several incentive programs aimed at employers, industry consultations suggest these have not yet been implemented or are otherwise ineffective. A common priority outlined across all four countries relates to incentives for companies to organize industry apprenticeships for students. Implemented in the Philippines through the government's Dual Training System and JobStart programs, such policies have not yet been fully implemented in the other countries. In Indonesia, for example, the government is currently developing detailed implementation arrangements for tax incentives for student apprenticeships announced in July 2019.[33] Such incentives are similarly in the planning stages in Cambodia and Viet Nam.

Further scope therefore exists to catalyze investment outside of government to develop workforce skills in all four countries. Possible approaches that emulate international best practice include establishing worker training incentives for firms, issuing training credits to stimulate increased training uptake by workers, and developing affordable short-term and high-impact courses for skills in demand under 4IR (footnote 23).

Foster collaboration between governments, industry, and civil society on nationwide training frameworks. To form such frameworks for 4IR, governments must consult and engage extensively with industry and civil society on the skills and jobs in demand. Across the four countries, this policy area has enjoyed stronger focus than others, with the Philippines assessed as demonstrating a *strong* focus and the other three countries as *moderate* (Figure 22).

The *strong* focus in the Philippines entails involving industry in both developing training programs for workers and formulating skills assessment and certification frameworks. The Governments of Cambodia, Indonesia, and Viet Nam are also emphasizing collaboration with employers, educators, and training institutions on skills development and establishing "innovation centers," or physical hubs for demonstrating new technologies to stimulate company adoption and facilitate worker training. Mandatory industry-led student apprenticeship programs are another common thread across all four countries. However, most of these efforts, particularly those in Cambodia and Viet Nam, have not yet been adapted for 4IR.

Other focus countries could emulate government collaboration with industry in the Philippines to publish a biannually updated report identifying key skills and jobs in emerging industries, as well as opportunities for workers to be trained in them.[34] Another good model is Indonesia's program developing innovation centers through an industry–government–research partnership. The centers will showcase

---

[31] J. W. Lee. 2016. How Can Asia Close Its Emerging Skills Gap? WEF Regional Agenda.
[32] WEF. 2018. *The Future of Jobs Report 2018*.
[33] Based on consultation with the Ministry of Industry in July 2019.
[34] Government of the Philippines, Department of Labor Employment. 2019. *JobsFit 2022 —Labor Market Information Report*.

"mini plants" to demonstrate 4IR technologies applicable in key Indonesian industries. Plans call for the development of four centers over the next few years in polytechnics located in four different cities, to ensure even geographical distribution and maximize learning opportunities for students.[35]

All four countries could do more to align current government–industry–institute collaboration to develop workforce skills that match more closely with 4IR, in particular identifying concrete mechanisms and programs where 4IR-specific knowhow and skills could be honed.

Create New Flexible Qualification Pathways

Establish effective lifelong learning models. An ever-evolving technology landscape demands a culture of lifelong learning, to make it possible to develop an adaptable and nimble workforce able to meet changing needs in the labor market. This is a critical policy area for the four countries, particularly given their relatively low rates of education attainment. In 2017, for example, 31% of Cambodia's labor force had not graduated from primary school, and 70% of Indonesia's labor force had graduated only from senior secondary school.[36] The Philippines and Viet Nam have focused on establishing lifelong learning models, with their policy focus in this area ranked *moderate*; the focus in Cambodia and Indonesia is ranked *weak* (Figure 22).

Both the Philippines and Viet Nam have established national policies on lifelong learning, under which community-based learning opportunities and skills development pathways for individuals have been developed. Though they have not yet embedded specific 4IR focuses, these are good platforms for developing future 4IR courses and efforts to build awareness. Meanwhile, lifelong learning policies appear nascent at best in Cambodia and Indonesia, focused on conventional skills training for job seekers and expanding access to education for individuals who missed out on them in their youth.

Viet Nam in particular offers a strong model that the other countries could adopt. The Viet Nam Association for Learning Promotion advocates and initiates lifelong learning. In operation throughout the country since 1996, with a focus on prioritizing family and adult learning, the association has developed a strong network of local learning centers where the general public may attend a variety of training courses. In addition, the organization conducts its own research and consults for the government, including as a major contributor to the National Framework for Building a Learning Society.[37]

Beyond expanding access to higher education and conventional skills training courses, each focus country could do more to equip its workforce with at least a basic awareness of 4IR and the necessary skills.

Ensure the agility of education and training curricula and their relevance to emerging skill needs. Educational curricula from the primary to the tertiary level need to be relevant to the emerging needs of a 4IR economy, including both technological skills and soft skills such as creativity and problem-solving.

---

[35] The four planned innovation centers will feature technologies relevant to local economies: F&B and automotive manufacturing in Jakarta, textile manufacturing in Bandung, F&B processing in Yogyakarta, agricultural automation in Makassar, and data analytics in Denpasar. Source: Consultation with the Ministry of Industry in July 2019.
[36] Government of Cambodia, National Institute of Statistics. 2017. *Cambodia Socio-Economic Survey 2017*; *Jakarta Post*. 2016. Five Plans to Upskill Indonesia's Workforce. 4 May.
[37] UNESCO (United Nations Educational, Scientific and Cultural Organization) Institute for Lifelong Learning. 2017. *Lifelong Learning in Transformation: Promising Practices in Southeast Asia.* Paris: UNESCO.

Although all four countries pursue a range of policies to make their curricula more responsive to industry needs, such as Indonesia encouraging or mandating industry–institution collaboration, studies and stakeholder consultations found rigidity in curricula. This was particularly the case in Cambodia, Indonesia, and the Philippines, where the focus on this area is assessed to be *weak* (Figure 22). In the Philippines, for example, slow approval processes in the Commission on Higher Education and high setup costs in implementing curriculum changes have deterred many institutions.[38] In Cambodia, stakeholder consultations revealed that industry–institution partnerships appeared to materialize only for larger, better-resourced institutes.

Viet Nam, on the other hand, is assessed as having a *strong* approach in this area (Figure 22). The government's National Strategy for 4IR outlines a series of policies to adjust educational curricula to align with 4IR.[39] The country is adopting a multifaceted approach that can be incorporated within vocational curricula online training programs for 4IR, including on technology management, working with international development partners to introduce new 4IR equipment in vocational training programs, and embedding a strong focus on soft skills such as language and communication skills. These are practices that the other three focus countries could adopt.

Encourage a focus on skills, not just formal qualifications, in recruitment and national labor market strategies. A focus on flexible skills qualification is essential to ensuring the readiness of workers for the 4IR economy, albeit building on traditional skills qualification frameworks.[40] Multiple industry stakeholders consulted in each of the four countries mentioned a particular need to change attitudes among job seekers and employers with respect to vocational skills.[41]

Among the focus countries, Indonesia appears to have developed the most concrete mechanisms to enable the hiring of individuals lacking educational qualifications. It has abolished minimum education qualifications for enrollment in vocational training centers[42] and issued "certificates of competency" that, through competence-testing, recognize the work-relevant skills of individuals with work experience but no educational qualifications.[43] However, all four countries still strongly emphasize traditional qualifications attained through the education system, as opposed to work experience and skills thus gained. Obtaining skills certificates in all four countries still often requires competency assessments and, except in Indonesia, past education attainment. Indonesia's exceptional status here earns it a *moderate* rating on this focus; the other countries are rated *weak* (Figure 22).

With 4IR putting large segments of working populations at risk of displacement, it is important for these countries to develop more flexible qualifications for employment, reflected in government labor market strategies and employers' recruitment practices.

---

[38] A. C. Orbeta, K. G. Gonzales, and S. F. S Cortes. 2016. *Are Higher Education Institutions Responsive to Changes in the Labor Market?* Discussion Paper 2016-08. Quezon City: PIDS.

[39] Central Institute for Economic Management (CIEM). 2019. Draft National Strategy for 4IR (unpublished). Obtained from CIEM in August 2019.

[40] J. S. Ng. 2018. Focus on Skills, Not Paper Qualifications, to Embrace Technological Change: Lawrence Wong. *Straits Times.* 5 May.

[41] Based on consultation with industry stakeholders in July 2019.

[42] *Jakarta Post.* 2016. Five Plans to Upskill Indonesia's Workforce. 4 May.

[43] Lee Kuan Yew School of Public Policy and Microsoft. 2016. *Technical and Vocational Education and Training in Indonesia: Challenges and Opportunities for the Future.*

Build Inclusive Labor Markets to Extend Industry 4.0 Benefits to All Workers

Allow underserved groups to benefit from 4IR. While 4IR promises to bring about greater productivity and wealth, it could just as easily exacerbate existing vulnerability among labor market participants with less technological knowhow. This is potentially a great risk in these four countries, where labor markets have traditionally failed women, the young, and rural workers. Yet governments do not appear to be focusing strongly on building more inclusive labor markets to provide underserved groups with better opportunities, let alone on training them in preparation for 4IR.

The Philippines is assessed with a *moderate* focus in this area; the other three countries are assessed as *weak* (Figure 22). A common action seen across all four countries is basic skills training for underserved communities. These efforts come largely from nongovernment organizations and private companies, however, and often occur on a limited scale.

Several programs in the Philippines represent positive models that the other three countries could consider for adoption. One is JobStart Philippines, which aims to shorten job searches for young workers by providing them with industry-relevant skills through training courses and internships, as well as employment facilitation services.[44] Another initiative is the Online Program of the Technical Education and Skills Development Authority (TESDA), which provides free online technical and vocational education and training (TVET) courses to individuals unable to pursue training because of financial and/or geographic hurdles. In its first 4 years, the program acquired 1.1 million registered users, 60% of them female.[45] Although these programs have not yet acquired a 4IR focus, they are ready platforms for this purpose.

Across all four countries, governments could develop larger and better-targeted interventions to ensure vulnerable segments of the population have access to skills training for 4IR.

Create social protection mechanisms for workers taking on flexible forms of labor. A global feature of 4IR is the emergence of temporary and flexible contracting of labor, often supported by the rise of sharing economy platforms such as the car service Grab and the online rental marketplace, Airbnb. Also termed "on-demand" or "gig economy" workers, these are freelancers who typically find work through online talent platforms or sharing economy applications, performing tasks for a wide variety of customers.[46] However, while high-income economies globally work to adapt to this new mode of work, backed up by their entrenched social protections designed for large, stable workforces, governments in these four countries still struggle to extend social protection to all segments of the workforce, flexible or not. Given the lack of any social protection in these countries, all four are assessed to have *weak* approaches in this area (Figure 22).

This is a critical problem, as the proliferation of gig economy or flexible workers is a trend in all four countries. The Philippines ranks sixth in the world in terms of fast-growing gig markets and is the fifth largest supplier of online labor, with at least 2% of the population working freelance.[47] Drivers of the ride-hailing service Gojek in Indonesia grew rapidly from 20 motorbike drivers when the company was founded in 2010 to over 1 million in 2018.[48]

---

[44] Government of the Philippines, TESDA. 2018. *National Technical Education and Skills Development Plan*; Government of the Philippines, Department of Labor and Employment. 2019. *JobStart Philippines Program*; ADB. 2018. *Social Protection Brief: Reducing Youth Not in Employment, Education or Training through JobStart Philippines*. Manila.
[45] Government of the Philippines, TESDA. 2018. *National Technical Education and Skills Development Plan*.
[46] Microsoft. 2018. *The Future Computed*.
[47] Payoneer. 2019. *The Global Gig Economy Index: Q2 2019*; L. Hasnan. 2019. Philippines's Fast-Growing Gig Economy. *ASEAN Post*. 21 February; Oxford Internet Institute. 2019. *Online Labour Index*.
[48] Gojek. https://www.gojek.com/sg/about/.

Such workers are increasing at risk socioeconomically as a result of the lack of social protection mechanisms. For example, 58% of freelancers in four ASEAN markets, including Indonesia and the Philippines, have experienced clients failing to pay them.[49] While Indonesia's Gojek drivers have benefited from more employment and higher incomes, they work up to 13 hours per day, well above the legal maximum of 8 hours, and lack minimum wage guarantees, insurance, and collective bargaining arrangements.[50]

Assessment of Implementation Approach

The study assessed the implementation of 4IR strategies for jobs and skills in each of the four countries against three dimensions that are crucial for successfully driving policy actions: clarity and robustness of plans, strength of stakeholder coordination, and alignment of financing and incentives.[51] These dimensions are further divided into nine implementation considerations for assessment (Figure 23). Each implementation consideration is rated *strong, moderate,* or *weak* according to how effective it is in each country.

With the development of national 4IR strategies at a nascent stage in all four countries, many areas of implementation require strengthening. While 4IR strategies in Cambodia and Indonesia appear to enjoy clearly articulated 4IR economic objectives and strong evidence bases in international and local data, in all countries the strength of coordination across and within stakeholder groups appears to be *weak,* as does the alignment of financing and incentives for skills development.

Clarity and Robustness of Plans

The starting point for successful implementation is to ensure a vision that is both realistic and clear, and that skills policy is tightly integrated into the overall 4IR strategy. Only Indonesia among the four countries currently has a clearly articulated vision for 4IR, though other country plans are being developed. None of the four countries has integrated its skills and employment strategy into its 4IR strategy.

Clarity of 4IR Vision

As Figure 23 shows, 4IR vision appears to be clearest in Indonesia, which has a *strong* rating, followed by Cambodia rated *moderate,* and the Philippines and Viet Nam rated *weak*.

The Making Indonesia 4.0 strategy offers a clearly articulated 4IR vision with specific and quantifiable targets that enable 4IR to benefit the economy. Viewed as instrumental to achieving the country's goal of becoming 1 of the 10 largest economies globally by 2030, 4IR is envisioned to deliver three economic outcomes: boosting net exports as a percentage of gross domestic product (GDP) by 13 times to reach 10%; doubling current labor productivity; and increasing the share of R&D spending in GDP by a factor of 7, from its current 0.3% to 2.0%.[52]

---

[49] Markets include Indonesia, the Philippines, Singapore, and Viet Nam. M. O'Malley. 2018. *PayPal Releases Global Freelancer Insights.* PayPal Stories; L. Hasnan. 2019. Philippines's Fast-Growing Gig Economy. *ASEAN Post.* 21 February.
[50] D. W. P. Yasih and A. R. Alamsyah. 2018. Can Grab and Gojek Drivers in Indonesia Build a Solid Union? *The Conversation.* 18 April.
[51] Based on AlphaBeta research of 4IR strategies, plus insights from past public sector research, including M. Barber. 2007. *Instruction to Deliver: Fighting to Transform Britain's Public Services.* London: Methueun; E. Daly and S. Singham. 2012. Delivery 2.0: The New Challenge for Governments. *McKinsey & Company.* 1 September.
[52] Ministry of Industry of the Republic of Indonesia. 2018. *Making Indonesia 4.0.*

Cambodia recently laid out a broad vision for 4IR in the Cambodia Trade Integration Strategy, which aspires to leapfrog from the current Second Industrial Revolution environment toward 4IR.[53] Though the country has yet to develop more detailed implementation strategies, this document is a good starting point.

Meanwhile, neither the Philippines nor Viet Nam have developed an explicit 4IR strategy. In the Philippines, articulation of a 4IR vision remains absent from national policies such as the Harmonized National R&D Agenda, 2017–2022 of the Department of Science and Technology. The Viet Nam national strategy for 4IR is still in development.[54] Both countries could consider positive examples on formulating 4IR visions from Cambodia and Indonesia.

Integration of Employment and Skills and 4IR Policy
This appears to be *weak* in the four countries, with 4IR and related policies largely separate from national skills and employment strategies. Even in Indonesia, where upgrading human capital is a highlighted priority under the Making Indonesia 4.0 strategy, policy analysis revealed only limited links with policies for skills development. In addition, 4IR and skills policies have different sets of priority industries.[55]

The Philippines has been assessed as having a *moderate* focus, as compared with a *weak* focus in the other countries (Figure 23). This is attributed to the TESDA National Technical Education and Skills Development Plan, 2018–2022, which considers the impacts of 4IR on jobs and skills and incorporates them into the national skills policy.[56] This is a positive practice that the other three countries could emulate.

Forward-Looking Plan Incorporating 4IR Trends
It is critical that the national 4IR strategy consider 4IR trends—either global or, if discernable, local—that affect potential improvements in labor productivity and costs. Cambodia and Indonesia are both assessed to have developed *strong* approaches to this, with the approach in Viet Nam rated *moderate* and that in the Philippines *weak* (Figure 23).

A strength in the approaches of both Cambodia and Indonesia relates to detailed analysis of international studies on 4IR trends and readiness, with clearly stated insights on how they should inform national 4IR policies. Cambodia has developed a series of strategic recommendations to address current deficiencies in its digital infrastructure and regulatory structure, based on a compilation of findings from five studies on the 4IR readiness of countries globally.[57] Similarly, the Making Indonesia 4.0 strategy leverages a series of international studies of 4IR technologies and their productivity-enhancing potential to create a shortlist of national economic targets for 4IR (footnote 52).

---

[53] Mekong Strategy Partners and Raintree Development. 2018. *Cambodia's Vibrant Startup Ecosystem.*
[54] Government of the Philippines, Department of Science and Technology. 2017. *Harmonized National Research and Development Agenda, 2017–2022.*
[55] Making Indonesia 4.0 prioritizes F&B manufacturing, automotive manufacturing, textiles and apparel, chemicals, and electronics, but national employment and skills strategies championed by the Coordinating Ministry of Human Resource prioritize manufacturing, agribusiness, tourism, health, migrant workers, and the digital economy. Government of Indonesia, Ministry of Industry. 2018. *Making Indonesia 4.0*; consultation with the Ministry of Manpower in July 2019.
[56] The seven industries are tourism; construction; ICT and IT-BPO; transport, communications, and storage; agriculture, fisheries, and forestry (including food manufacturing); manufacturing (including electronics); and health, wellness, and other social services. Government of the Philippines, TESDA. 2018. *National Technical Education and Skills Development Plan.*
[57] The five indexes are the World Economic Forum (WEF) Global Competitiveness Index, 2017–2018; Cornell University, INSEAD, and the World Intellectual Property Organization Global Innovation Index, 2017; the Danish Institute of Industry Global Industry 4.0 Readiness Index, 2016; the WEF Networked Readiness Index, 2016; and the KPMG Change Readiness Index, 2017. Government of Cambodia, Ministry of Commerce. 2019. *Cambodia Trade Integration Strategy 2019–2023.*

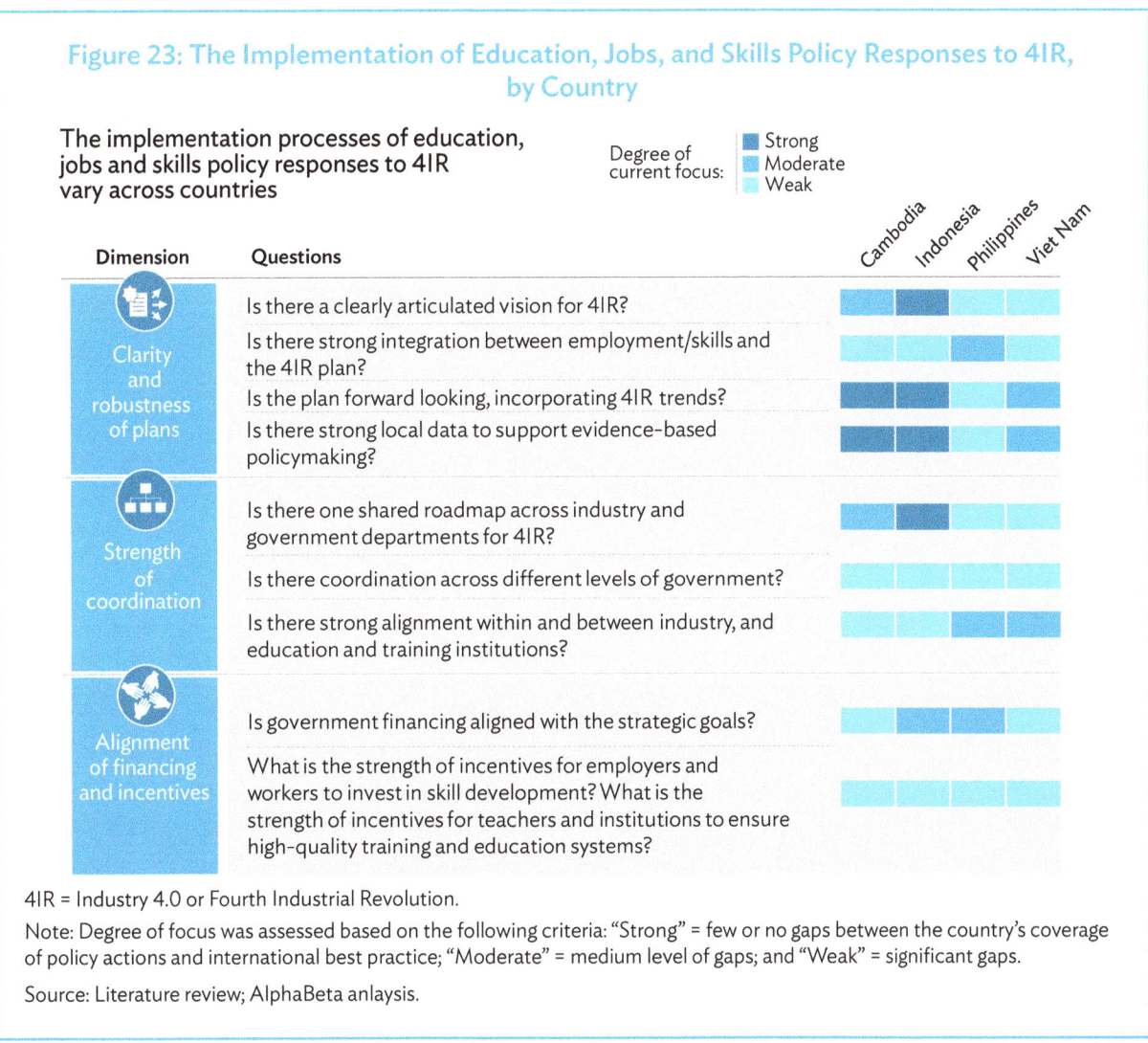

Figure 23: The Implementation of Education, Jobs, and Skills Policy Responses to 4IR, by Country

4IR = Industry 4.0 or Fourth Industrial Revolution.
Note: Degree of focus was assessed based on the following criteria: "Strong" = few or no gaps between the country's coverage of policy actions and international best practice; "Moderate" = medium level of gaps; and "Weak" = significant gaps.
Source: Literature review; AlphaBeta anlaysis.

Evidence-Based Policymaking Supported by Local Data
For 4IR strategies to achieve outcomes in line with national needs, policymaking must be supported by a local evidence base. The availability of local evidence varies across the four countries. As Figure 23 shows, Cambodia and Indonesia are rated *strong* in this area, Viet Nam *moderate*, and the Philippines *weak*.

In both Cambodia and Indonesia, thorough reviews of the readiness of key sectors for 4IR have been conducted to analyze the productivity potential of new technologies, the probability of firms adopting them, and potential barriers to adoption that the strategy would need to address.[58] Local firm and wage data were analyzed and surveys were conducted to distill these insights; in Indonesia, a detailed benchmarking study identified performance gaps between Indonesia and global and regional leaders.

---

[58] Government of Cambodia, Ministry of Commerce. 2019. *Cambodia Trade Integration Strategy 2019-2023*. Government of Indonesia, Ministry of Industry. 2018. *Making Indonesia 4.0*.

Conversely, 4IR-relevant strategies in the Philippines and Viet Nam rely on a very limited evidence base, with insights coming largely from secondary knowledge sources and international contexts.

Strength of Coordination

Alignment and clarity on the 4IR strategy at all relevant levels of government is crucial to its success. Likewise, strong coordination is necessary between industry and training institutions, but the focus countries appear to lack a unified 4IR road map. Coordination between ministries and different levels of government also appears to be limited.

A Shared 4IR Road map across Industry and Government

The existence of a single shared 4IR road map is often a strong indication of how coordinated a country's 4IR-related strategies are across the various government ministries that oversee policy. The development of Making Indonesia 4.0 and how it is being referenced across all government ministries demonstrates Indonesia's *strong* approach in this area (Figure 23). Cambodia is observed to have a *moderate* approach by virtue of its 4IR policy enunciated in the recently launched Cambodia Trade Integration Strategy—though it remains to be seen how this will dovetail with the upcoming Cambodia Digital Economy Policy. In the Philippines and Viet Nam, *weak* approaches are observed, with only scattered policies that relate to 4IR, though in Viet Nam a national document is under development.

Coordination across Government Ministries and Levels

All four countries are rated *weak* in this area (Figure 23). Coordination is lacking not only among government departments and ministries but also across different levels of government. Stakeholder consultations reveal that coordination between government departments has been limited and that interministerial platforms have thus far failed to produce a unified and coordinated policy on 4IR in any of the countries studied. In Indonesia, where one key 4IR road map has been developed, it has currency only in the Ministry of Industry.

Regarding coordination across levels of government, national plans often fail to translate directly into local implementation. A survey of 125 vocational high schools in Indonesia found that while national policy to foster institute–industry collaboration had succeeded in establishing initial partnership agreements between schools and companies, the follow-through was weak, with discussions not affecting curricula.[59] Discussions with industry stakeholders revealed that national government plans to improve vocational training had rarely trickled down to local schools, for lack of district vocational committees.[60]

Alignment of Education and Training Institutions with Industry

Alignment within and between these stakeholder groups has taken place to varying extents in the four countries. Alignment on pertinent issues such as critical skills required for 4IR, the relevance of educational and training curricula, and qualifications and skills certification systems appears to be uneven across industries, companies, and institutions. Consultations in country reveal that collaborative approaches tend to be more common in larger, better-resourced industry associations, companies, and institutions. The Philippines and Viet Nam are both assessed as *moderate* in their focus; Indonesia and Cambodia are assessed as *weak* in their focus (Figure 23).

---

[59] M. B. Triyono and D. E. Murniai. 2018. Alignment of the Curriculum to the Development of the Industrial World (Revitalization Program of Vocational High Schools in Indonesia). *TVET-Online*.

[60] Based on consultation with the Indonesian Chamber of Commerce and Industry in July 2019.

Some positive practices emerge. One is the IT and Business Process Association of the Philippines (IBPAP), which routinely undertakes studies on the skills landscape for the information technology and business process outsourcing (IT-BPO) sector and recommends to member companies how to recruit and develop talent for the digital economy.[61] IBPAP also collaborates with training institutions and government agencies to embed curricula and courses within private and public TVET curricula that IT-BPO employers deem critical for the 4IR economy.[62] In Viet Nam, the Hanoi College for Electro-Mechanics holds an annual meeting for enterprise partners to point out weaknesses and gaps in its skills training, with a consistent focus on exploring opportunities to involve the private sector more in training.[63]

Alignment of Financing and Incentives

For jobs and skills policies to successfully mitigate the potential negative impacts of 4IR, funding and incentives need to be well-aligned and ensure that all stakeholders contribute to skills development. While government financing is somewhat aligned with worker training priorities, R&D expenditure appears to be low in all four countries. Incentives for employers and workers to contribute to skills development also appear *weak* in each country.

Alignment of Government Financing with Strategic Goals

The financing commitments of governments in the four countries vary regarding the strategic goals outlined for 4IR. They are assessed as *moderate* in Indonesia and the Philippines but *weak* in Viet Nam and Cambodia (Figure 23).

Strategies relevant to 4IR in both Indonesia and the Philippines have been backed up with government financing commitments. In line with the goal of the Government of the Philippines to improve the quality and reach of TVET training, the national budget allocated to TESDA—the national TVET authority—nearly doubled from $150 million in 2018 to $290 million in 2019.[64] Similarly, the Government of Indonesia announced in 2019 that it had budgeted $726 million for a "pre-work card" scheme, which aims to provide training credit to 2 million workers starting in 2020.[65] Such financing commitments are substantial, but it remains to be seen if the money will indeed be deployed and the degree to which it will achieve the intended outcomes.

Strength of Incentives for Employers, Workers, and Other Stakeholders

Incentives for various stakeholder groups and their ability to help develop workforce skills are assessed as *weak* across all four countries (Figure 23). This is a particular area of concern, as it reduces the rate at which workers acquire skills and disproportionately burdens government coffers toward facilitating upskilling to meet 4IR needs. Stakeholder consultations with governments and training institutions confirm that the current model of government funding for skills development is unsustainable. Beyond broadly announced tax incentives for firms that undertake worker training—which have not been implemented except in the Philippines—incentives to induce employers and workers to invest in training are notable by their absence.

---

[61] An example study is IBPAP (IT and Business Process Management Association of the Philippines). 2014. *Talent Deep Dive: An Analysis of Talent Availability for the Information Technology and Business Process Management Industry in 10 Provinces in the Philippines*.
[62] Based on consultation with IBPAP in July 2019.
[63] Based on stakeholder discussions in July 2019.
[64] Government of the Philippines, Department of Budget and Management. 2019. *TESDA Budget Nearly Doubles in 2019*. Press Release.
[65] M. A. Iswara and M. I. Gorbiano. 2019. Jokowi's Preemployment Card Program under Scrutiny. *Jakarta Post*. 12 August.

Also assessed were incentives to improve teaching quality and for students to attend school. In all four countries, stakeholders often cited poor teaching quality as a key concern, pointing to a lack of professional development incentives for talented individuals with industry or 4IR experience to become teachers. Cambodia in particular struggles with low rates of basic education attainment as well as weak incentives for students to attend school. High dropout rates in primary and lower-secondary school are attributed to the limited wage premium for secondary education over primary education, which encourages low-income households to pull their children out of school for work.[66]

---

[66] ADB. 2015. *Cambodia: Addressing the Skills Gap*. Manila.

CHAPTER 4
The Way Forward

The three preceding chapters have highlighted the challenges facing the four focus countries—Cambodia, Indonesia, the Philippines, and Viet Nam—in relation to Industry 4.0 (4IR). This chapter summarizes them and offers several recommendations for addressing these challenges based on best practice in other countries.

The COVID-19 Effect

The study was undertaken and completed prior to the spread of coronavirus disease (COVID-19), which has caused unprecedented disruptions to labor markets and to the activities of the workforce across the world. This study's policy recommendations and strategies to strengthen widespread digital capabilities, online or distance learning, digital platforms, education technology, and simulation-based learning have become all the more relevant in the aftermath of COVID-19. The key approaches discussed bear great relevance in the current context of countries experiencing nationwide closures of schools and training institutes. The expectation is also that, after COVID-19, there will be operating procedures in place that will constitute a "new normal" that entails far more digital capabilities in the workplace. Hence, the findings of this study and the follow-on policy directions are timely, and crucial to facilitating a sustainable COVID-19 recovery strategy.

The eight sectors chosen for the study across the four countries have been adversely affected. In food and beverage (F&B) and agro-processing, the expectation is that there will be lasting shifts in consumer behavior in the COVID-19 response. Food retailers are likely to scale up e-commerce. The logistics part of the sector—storing, transporting, and delivering—is likely to become more tech-oriented, calling for new skills and talent.

Tourism worldwide has more or less ground to a halt as a result of COVID-19. The scale of cancellations and other disruptions calls out for greater use of digital tools and capabilities to orient the sector to a future world.

Workers in garments manufacturing have suffered massive layoffs, with factories closing down as a result of internal supply constraints and external demand shocks because of COVID-19.

The information technology and business process outsourcing (IT-BPO) sector has seen widespread disruptions to business operations as a result of COVID-19; however, the expectation is that there will be lasting shifts in business practices that will embody greater use of digital collaborative tools with cybersecurity and management following the COVID-19 response.

In the auto and electronics industries, recovery will entail embracing digital supply chains and launching digital sales and marketing initiatives.

More broadly, the logistics sector is expected to experience a significant upswing after COVID-19 arising from the growth in e-commerce and the changing nature of retail business owing to the pandemic. A recovery strategy will entail embracing digital supply chains and launching digital sales and marketing initiatives. Hence, upskilling and reskilling in 4IR-related occupations is even more urgent for the revival of the economy and economic stimulus needed after COVID-19.

This study does not address the implications of COVID-19 in the countries of focus; however, the policy directions and recommended future investments for higher-order skills, particularly in the digital domain, are eminently suitable for the countries to reimagine new beginnings for each of the two sectors discussed.

Facing the Four Countries

Figure 24 recaps the challenges facing the four countries, as determined in the sector analysis in Chapter 1, the analysis of training institute surveys in Chapter 2, and the policy assessment in Chapter 3.

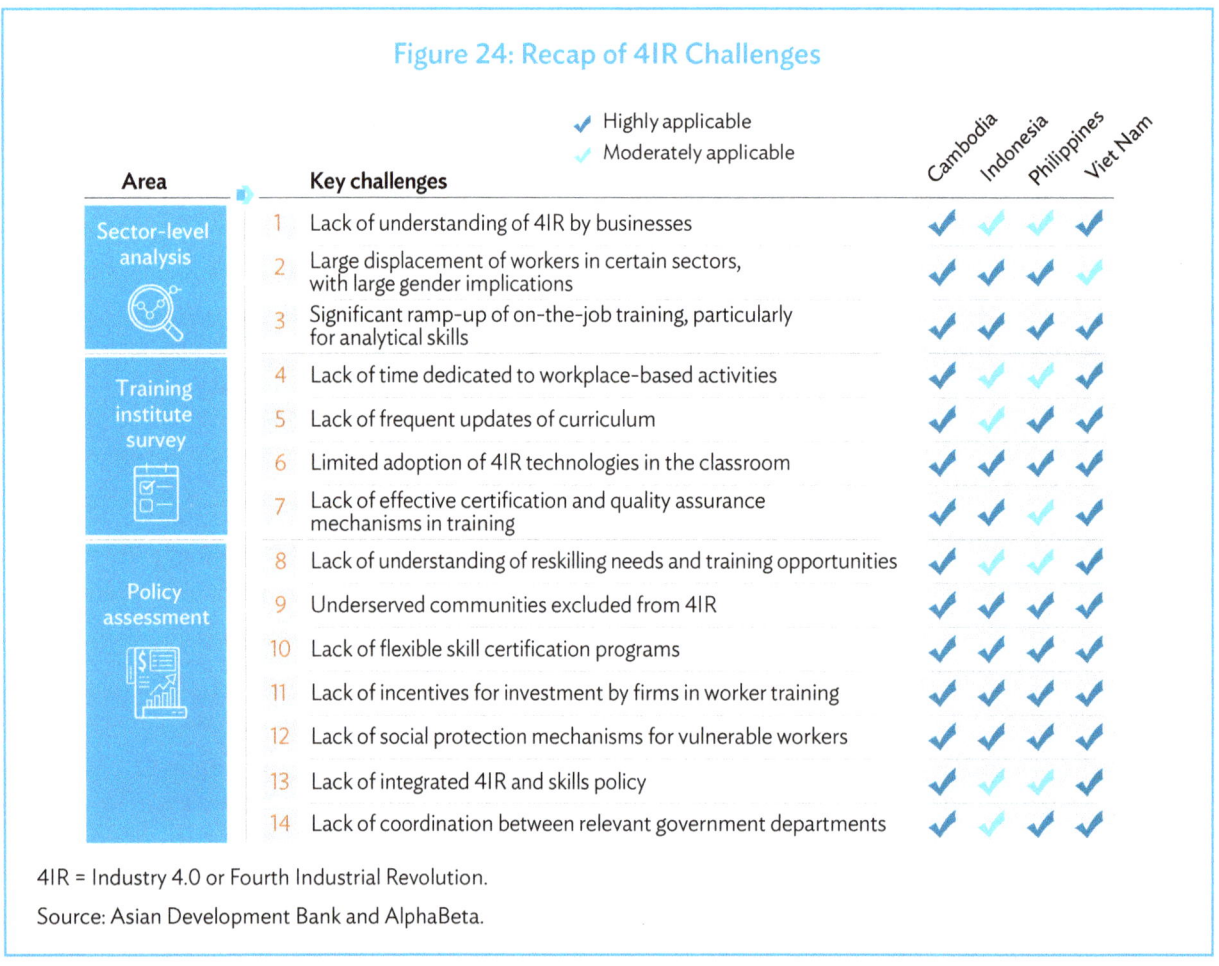

Figure 24: Recap of 4IR Challenges

4IR = Industry 4.0 or Fourth Industrial Revolution.
Source: Asian Development Bank and AlphaBeta.

Recommendations to Address Challenges

The four focus countries could strengthen their approaches to 4IR in a number of areas. The table presents several recommendations that draw on international best practices to strengthen current approaches in terms of both policy scope and implementation. The recommendations are applicable across all four countries.

Examples of 4IR Skills-Related Best Practices from Around the World

No	Recommendation	Common Challenges	Examples of Countries where Recommendation Implemented
1	Develop 4IR transformation road maps for key sectors	• Lack of understanding of 4IR by businesses • Large displacement of workers in certain sectors, with large gender implications • Lack of understanding of reskilling needs and training opportunities • Lack of integrated 4IR and skills policy • Lack of coordination between relevant government departments	Australia, Singapore
2	Develop a series of industry-led TVET programs targeting skills for 4IR	• Lack of effective certification and quality assurance mechanisms in training • Significant ramp-up of on-the-job training, particularly for analytical skills • Lack of time dedicated to workplace-based activities • Lack of frequent updates of curriculum	Denmark, Finland, France, Germany, India, Norway, Switzerland
3	Upgrade training delivery through 4IR technology in classrooms and training facilities	• Limited adoption of 4IR technologies in the classroom	South Africa
4	Develop flexible and modular skill certification programs	• Lack of flexible skill certification programs	Malaysia
5	Formulate new approaches and measures to strengthen inclusion and social protection in the context of 4IR	• Underserved communities excluded from 4IR • Lack of social protection mechanisms for vulnerable workers	Australia, Japan, Malaysia, Republic of Korea
6	Implement an incentive scheme for firms to train employees for 4IR	• Lack of incentives for investment by firms in worker training	Malaysia, Singapore

4IR = Industry 4.0 or Fourth Industrial Revolution.
Source: Asian Development Bank and AlphaBeta.

> **Box 6: Singapore's Industry Transformation Maps**
>
> A dedicated body called the Future Economy Council prepares Singapore's Industry 4.0 industry transformation maps (ITMs). Chaired by the deputy prime minister, the council has representatives from government, industry, unions, and educational and training institutes.[a] Each ITM charts 4IR technology adoption for a particular industry.[b] To ensure coordination and accountability within the government, each ITM is championed by the government agency whose purview is most relevant to the sector (footnote b). For example, the ITM for manufacturing is led by the Economic Development Agency, whereas the Building and Construction Authority leads that for the built environment.
>
> A key component of each ITM is its skills framework. Co-created by actors in industry, government, and civil society, the framework provides information on career pathways, the existing and emerging skills required for different occupations, and reskilling options for different sectors. It also lists training programs for upgrading skills. By virtue of its multiple-stakeholder nature, this framework is intended to benefit not just workers but also employers, by enabling them to identify emerging skills needs for their workers and enhance their efforts to attract and retain talent; providers of training, by giving them better insights into emerging skill trains and how best to target critical skill gaps through appropriate courses; and students, by facilitating informed decisions on study choice in line with their career aspirations. A 2018 survey of over 700 firms in Singapore found that 36% of them used ITMs to improve their talent pipeline and guide their efforts to address manpower shortages.[c]
>
> [a] Government of Singapore, Ministry of Education. 2016. *Formation of the Council for Skills, Innovation, and Productivity.* Press Release.
> [b] Government of Singapore, Ministry of Trade and Industry. 2017. *Industry Transformation Maps.* Media Factsheet.
> [c] S. K. Tang. 2019. Singapore Businesses Not Investing Enough in Employee Training: SBF Survey. *Channel News Asia.* 17 January.
>
> Source: Asian Development Bank and AlphaBeta.

Recommendation 1: Develop Industry 4.0 transformation road maps for key sectors.

An implementation strategy that includes both technology adoption and skills development is key to driving 4IR technological adoption in the four countries while ensuring that their workers acquire and upgrades skills to maximize productivity benefits and minimize job displacement. Government stakeholders consulted in workshops held in country were particularly concerned about how to ensure parallel development on both tracks. It is thus critical to consider a deliberate implementation strategy that embeds both focuses, particularly in Cambodia and Viet Nam, where existing policy frameworks currently reflect links between technology adoption and skills development only weakly. A starting point could be to develop, as in Singapore, industry transformation maps that provide information on technology impacts, career pathways, the skills required for different occupations, and reskilling options for different sectors (Box 6).[67]

Recommendation 2: Develop industry-led technical and vocational education and training programs that target skills for Industry 4.0.

The poor quality of TVET programs and their lack of industry relevance were identified in employer surveys covered in Chapter 1 and in training institute surveys covered in Chapter 2. A recommendation to make TVET programs stronger and more relevant is to have industry lead their development. Labor or manpower ministries could support this effort, working with industry associations and education

---
[67] SkillsFuture. 2019. Skills Framework.

> **Box 7: Connecting Students and Industry with Boot Camps**
>
> Industry needs appropriately trained recruits, and young job seekers need to be hired. Industry boot camps can connect the skills young job seekers offer to those sought by industry. The Generation Program develops programs focusing on four industries, with teaching facilities in 119 cities on six continents accepting applicants aged 18–29.[a] Among its features are direct contact with potential employers; trainee attributes matched with employer needs; courses that cover technical, behavioral, and mental skills; continuous monitoring and support during and after the program; and a substantial alumni network. There is a strong focus on equipping recruits with Industry 4.0 skills, such as digital marketing, web development, java programming, and cloud management. Program implementation, workspace, and instructors are usually provided in partnership with a local training institute.
>
> Since program inception, 31,600 people have been trained, with 80% of them finding jobs within 3 months of finishing the program and 65% of that group staying in the job for at least a year (footnote a). Employers rate program graduates as higher performing than their peers.[b]
>
> [a] *Generation Program*.
> [b] Asia Philanthropy Circle. 2017. *Catalysing Productive Livelihood: A Guide to Education Interventions with an Accelerated Path to Scale and Impact*.
>
> Source: Asian Development Bank and AlphaBeta.

institutions to scope such programs. Parameters would include training curricula, taking into account which 4IR technologies to teach and their duration; teacher recruitment and training; and applicant criteria. Toward firming these parameters, the formats of industry-led TVET programs reflecting international best practice may be considered. Some notable examples include industry boot camps run by McKinsey & Company's Generation Program, which operates across several countries (Box 7).

Recommendation 3: Upgrade training delivery through Industry 4.0 technology in classrooms and training facilities.

Surveys of training institutions drawn on in Chapter 2 reveal that, while many training institutions use some 4IR technologies such as online learning modules, only a few use a more complete suite of technologies that includes virtual or augmented reality. National stakeholder consultations in July and October 2019 revealed varying degrees of technology adoption by training institutions in the four countries, with better-resourced institutions taking up more technologies.

A range of new technologies could support 4IR instruction. Artificial intelligence (AI), for example, has been used to stimulate critical thinking by applying a virtual environment toward building and assessing higher-order inquiry skills.[68] AI-enabled immersive computer games have been applied to teaching science, technology, engineering, and mathematics in some schools in the United States.[69] As installing such technologies and equipment at every institution would be fiscally challenging, adopting blended learning approaches could help manage costs while maximizing benefits. Blended learning, which combines classroom and personalized online learning, has been demonstrated to be a highly cost-effective way to improve education outcomes while addressing gender inequality (Box 8).

---

[68] J. M. Spector and S. Ma. 2019. Inquiry and Critical Thinking Skills for the Next Generation: From Artificial Intelligence Back to Human Intelligence. *Smart Learning Environments*. 6 (8).
[69] D. J. Ketelhut et al. 2009. A Multi-User Virtual Environment for Building and Assessing Higher Order Inquiry Skills in Science. *British Journal of Educational Technology*. 20 December.

> **Box 8: Leveraging Technologies to Improve Education and Address Gender Inequality**
>
> Digital technologies have been shown to improve education quality while managing gender gaps starting from at an early age.
>
> The African School for Excellence, an affordable private secondary school in South Africa, deploys an innovative classroom model in which students rotate between teacher-facilitated lessons, peer learning in small groups, and individual work on computers supervised by trainee teachers. Using free online courses from sources such as Khan Academy, this blended learning approach innovatively reduces costs through its reliance on a smaller number of highly trained teachers, while enhancing education outcomes with its emphasis on personalized learning and small classes. Students in the school outperform the wealthiest students in South Africa by 2.3 times in mathematics and 1.4 times in English (in terms of average scores).[a] At the same time, the annual cost per student of $800 is low when compared with more typical South African costs of $1,400–$16,500 per year (footnote a).
>
> Such personalized and adaptive digital learning tools are beginning to show potential for bridging gender differences in students' attainment from a young age. onebillion, a London-based nonprofit organization focused on building scalable educational software for children, has launched the app onecourse, which delivers content and practice on a tablet. This app was found to prevent a gender gap in reading and mathematics skills from surfacing among Grade 1 students in Malawi, perhaps by overcoming sociocultural factors responsible for gaps in traditional classroom settings.[c]
>
> [a] Center for Universal Education at Brookings. 2019. *Learning to Leapfrog: Innovative Pedagogies to Transform Education.*
> [b] onebillion. *Onecourse: One App that Delivers Reading, Writing and Numeracy.*
> [c] Pathways for Prosperity Commission. 2019. *Positive Disruption: Health and Education in the Digital Age.*
>
> Source: Asian Development Bank and AlphaBeta.

Recommendation 4: Develop flexible and modular skills certification programs.

As Chapter 3 outlined, emphasis remains strong on traditional qualifications attained through formal education or competency assessments. It is recommended that each country explore the development of flexible skills certification programs that recognize skills acquired outside of traditional education channels. A positive example of such a system is the Malaysian Skills Certification Program, which grants skills certificates to advance the career prospects of workers who have acquired knowledge, experience, and skills in the workplace despite having no formal educational qualifications (Box 9). A starting point could be for each country to review with industry and training institutions how effective minimum educational qualifications and competency-based assessments are in current certification frameworks. These should be assessed in light of practical need for such qualifications, and the extent to which they adequately indicate competence in specific skills.

Recommendation 5: Formulate new approaches and measures to strengthen inclusion and social protection under Industry 4.0.

With few opportunities available to a substantial portion of low-income families and residents of rural areas, programs promoting inclusive skills development in all four countries are critical to ensuring that 4IR does not leave people behind. When targeting interventions, governments are recommended to identify vulnerable communities most at risk from 4IR and to work with community leaders. Interventions should train three types of workers—entry level, those at risk from job displacement, and workers in need of upskilling—using modern delivery mechanisms, including digital platforms and industry-recognized credentials. One possible approach is to provide online learning channels, as does

> ### Box 9: The Malaysian Skills Certification Program
>
> In Malaysia, individuals who lack formal educational qualifications can enter their desired careers through the Malaysian Skills Certification Program.
>
> Recognized by industry, this program awards Malaysian Skills certification at five different levels, the bottom three certificates, the fourth a diploma, and the fifth an advanced diploma.[a]
>
> These certificates are awarded across 22 sectors, as classified by the country's National Occupational Skills Standard.[b] Importantly, no formal educational qualifications are required—only the ability to speak and write in both Bahasa Melayu and English, and the need to have passed a lower skills certificate level before qualifying for higher certification in the same field (footnote a).
>
> Candidates may obtain certificates through three channels: training in institutions accredited by the Department of Skills Development; industry apprenticeships under the National Dual Training System; and sufficient accreditation of prior achievement, or evidence of past work experience and/or training (footnote a).
>
> These certificates are officially recognized and mapped to equivalent academic qualifications under the Malaysian Qualifications Framework. Companies refer to this framework when assessing job candidates without formal education but possessing the skills needed to excel at the job.[c]
>
> [a] Government of Malaysia, Department of Skills Development. *Malaysian Skill Certificate (SKM)*.
> [b] OECD (Organisation for Economic Co-operation and Development). 2012. *Skills Development Pathways in Asia*. Paris: OECD.
> [c] Government of Malaysia, Ministry of Higher Education, and Malaysian Qualifications Agency. 2011. *Malaysian Qualifications Framework*.
>
> Source: Asian Development Bank and AlphaBeta.

the Ministry of Higher Education in Malaysia, which encourages and supports universities' creation of open online courses mandated to be available to the general public.[70] Another approach is to target skills development programs to specific underserved groups. Yet another is to offer financial incentives for employers to train specific underserved communities, as does the Career-Up Josei-Kin Program in Japan by providing employers with subsidies for training individuals on less comprehensive contracts.[71]

Chapter 3 highlighted the lack of social protection for the rapidly growing number of workers on demand as a key concern. Several policy options to provide social protection to such workers should undergo cost–benefit analysis toward selecting promising schemes to pilot test for broader applicability. Policy approaches should be explored to enhance income security for casual workers, perhaps adopting an Australian policy that entitles workers on short-term contracts to an increment of 25% over workers doing the same job on staff.[72] Alternatively, governments can work with employers to champion corporate policies mandating income stability for such workers, using some of the innovative approaches available. Care.com, for example, is a platform for caregivers seeking work. It enables employers to contribute to their caregivers' benefits in much the same way that traditional corporate employers fund employee benefits.[73]

---

[70] United Nations Educational, Scientific and Cultural Organization (UNESCO) Institute for Lifelong Learning. 2017. *Lifelong Learning in Transformation: Promising Practices in Southeast Asia*.
[71] Organisation for Economic Co-operation and Development (OECD). 2017. *Financial Incentives for Steering Education and Training, Getting Skills Right*. Paris: OECD.
[72] OECD (Organisation for Economic Co-operation and Development). 2018. *The Future of Social Protection: What Works for Non-Standard Workers?* Paris.
[73] G. Bonoli. 2019. Ensuring Economic Security in the Gig Economy. *Business Times*, 13 March; Microsoft. 2018. *The Future Computed*.

Recommendation 6: Offer incentives for firms to train employees for Industry 4.0.

Despite the substantial productivity gains 4IR technologies could bring about (as Chapter 1 demonstrated), employer-led training efforts in the four countries remain limited. National surveys reveal that less than one-fifth of firms in Cambodia and less than a quarter of those in Indonesia provide formal training for their employees.[74] A survey conducted by the World Economic Forum (WEF) found that 4% more employers in the Philippines and 5% more in Viet Nam would rather hire new staff with the required skills than retrain existing workers, and that 74% in the Philippines and 68% in Viet Nam simply expect employees to pick up skills on the job.[75]

Three key sources of market failure could explain these low training rates, which relate to both information asymmetries about the benefits and availability of training and a lack of economic incentives for training:

(i) There are information asymmetries pertaining to a limited awareness of the need to take up new skills for 4IR, and even a lack of understanding of different types of 4IR technologies and their productivity benefits in some industries. In a recent survey to understand the attitudes of employers in Indonesia and the Philippines toward reskilling for AI, one of the most commonly cited reasons for not undergoing training courses was insufficient time (59% of employers in Indonesia and 44% in the Philippines), reflecting a lack of priority accorded to training. Further, in-country consultations and employer surveys across all four countries revealed a concerning lack of understanding of 4IR technologies and their productivity benefits (particularly in Cambodia's garment manufacturing industry and Viet Nam's agro-processing industry).

(ii) Another source of information asymmetry is the lack of awareness surrounding upskilling and reskilling opportunities. The same survey on attitudes toward training for AI revealed that employers in the Association of Southeast Asian Nations had limited understanding of such opportunities in their countries. Not knowing what courses their employees should take to skill up in AI knowhow was a commonly cited reason for not providing formal training to workers (about 40% of employers in Indonesia and the Philippines felt this way).[76] Similarly, in-country consultations with training institutions in each of the four countries revealed that, where there were relevant courses available, employers were generally unaware of them. In Cambodia, a national employer survey found that lack of information on courses and trainers was one of the key reasons behind low training rates.

(iii) Market-driven economic incentives for employer-led training efforts are weak as a result of thin budgets available for training as well as a strong reliance on short-term contracting in some labor markets. A national employer survey in Cambodia reflected that, although 72% of firms surveyed had developed training plans, three-quarters were unable to allocate budgets to these plans.[77] In the Philippines, the largest challenge facing surveyed business leaders in reskilling their workers for AI is not being able to afford training courses.[78] In Indonesia, it has been demonstrated that a strong reliance on short-term contracted workers has led to underinvestment in training by companies to invest in workers' skills development.[79]

---

[74] National Employment Agency, Cambodia. 2017. *Skills Shortages and Skills Gaps in the Cambodian Labour Market: Evidence from Employer Survey 2017*; J. W. Lee. 2016. *How can Asia Close its Emerging Skills Gap?* WEF Regional Agenda.
[75] WEF. 2018. *The Future of Jobs Report 2018*.
[76] Microsoft and International Data Corporation. 2018. *Artificial Intelligence to Nearly Double the Rate of Innovation in Asia Pacific by 2021*.
[77] Government of Cambodia, National Employment Agency. 2017. *Skills Shortages and Skills Gaps in the Cambodian Labour Market: Evidence from Employer Survey 2017*.
[78] Microsoft and International Data Corporation. 2018. *Digital Transformation to Contribute US$8 billion to the Philippines GDP by 2021*.
[79] E. Allen. 2016. Raising Indonesian Labor Productivity. *Nikkei Asian Review*. 9 August.

> **Box 10: Incentive Schemes in the Region for Training by Firms**
>
> The Government of Singapore provides subsidies to firms for employee training course fees and absentee payroll salary costs, with higher incentives awarded for courses that are government certified.[a] While subsidies for government-certified and "approved certifiable" courses cover 90%–95% of course fees, those for the latter have hourly caps. On the other hand, subsidies for noncertifiable courses are lower, at S$2 per hour of training. Absentee payroll funding covers up to 95% of the base salary. The Government of Malaysia's similar Skills Upgrading Program provides grants covering 70% of training fees paid by small and medium-sized enterprises for technical and soft skills.
>
> [a] Skillsfuture Singapore. 2019. *Funding Support for Employers*.
> [b] Microsoft and AlphaBeta. 2019. *Preparing for AI: The Implications of Artificial Intelligence for Jobs and Skills in Asian Economies*.
>
> Source: Asian Development Bank and AlphaBeta.

Given these challenges, it is critical to develop a set of support programs to encourage firms to invest in relevant 4IR training for their workers. Although all four countries have either implemented or plan to implement financial incentives such as tax breaks for employers to offer in-service worker training and student apprenticeships, little has been accomplished so far, and enforcement has been a challenge. Tax reductions of up to 50% offered to employers in the Philippines that participate in the Dual Training System, for example, have enjoyed only limited success because qualifying for them entails tedious administrative requirements.[80] Indonesia's announcement in mid-2019 of a 200% tax refund for company expenditures on student training and internships has also yet to be implemented, and local stakeholders stated that the biggest hurdle would be formalizing the program details, such as the required duration of apprenticeships, the scope of the training, and government enforcement mechanisms.[81] Cambodia has recently launched a skills development fund that is still nascent.[82]

This action involves developing appropriate incentive programs for firms to invest in worker skills development related to 4IR in four steps:

(i) identifying appropriate incentive programs for firms (Box 10 provides some international examples);
(ii) undertaking a holistic cost–benefit analysis of the incentive scheme and associated training programs (noting that such analyses of training programs carried out from the government's perspective have tended to focus largely on the direct economic costs of the program, while disregarding indirect economic benefits such as reduced welfare payments as training lowers unemployment rates);
(iii) piloting programs in a number of priority sectors (including building awareness of available training programs); and
(iv) scaling up the program to include other industries and incorporating lessons learned from the pilot.

---

[80] Government of the Philippines, TESDA. 2018. *National Technical Education and Skills Development Plan*; consultation with industry stakeholders in the Philippines in July 2019.
[81] Consultation with the Ministry of Industry in July 2019; *Jakarta Post*. 2019. Jokowi Issues Rule on Tax Deductions of Up to 300% of R&D Cost. 9 July.
[82] Consultations with the Center for Information and Statistics in October 2019 and the Council for the Development of Cambodia in July 2019.

Industry-specific priorities

While the above recommendations apply broadly across the focus industries and countries, a set of unique priorities should be considered for each industry when implementing the respective policy actions. These have been formed based on thorough in-country consultations with government officials, industry stakeholders, and representatives from training institutes.

- **Focus on addressing information and capability gaps in the manufacturing industries.** The employer surveys suggest that awareness of 4IR technology opportunities is more limited in manufacturing industries than in services industries. This could perhaps owe to the complexity and relative nascence of 4IR technologies in the manufacturing industries (e.g., Internet-of-Things-enabled "smart factories," collaborative robots, additive manufacturing) as compared with the services industries (e.g., established AI software or chatbot technologies for the IT-BPO industry, travel booking apps for tourism services). In particular, 4IR awareness levels among employers are low in Cambodia's garment manufacturing, Indonesia's F&B, and Viet Nam's agro-processing—as compared with services industries such as tourism in Cambodia and the IT-BPO industry in the Philippines. As such, a high priority must be placed on ensuring and enhancing employers' understanding of 4IR in the first stage of any of the recommended policy actions. For example, before developing the skills framework within the sector-specific 4IR transformation road maps (Recommendation 1), government and industry stakeholders will have to work with technology experts and align on the types of 4IR technologies applicable to the industry. It will also be important to cultivate this understanding in downstream employee training programs. In addition, there tend to be large knowledge gaps on 4IR technologies between large and small firms in the manufacturing industries. Many of the manufacturing firms analyzed have ecosystems characterized by a small number of larger companies (often local branches of or local factories contracted by multinational companies) and many smaller micro, small, and medium-sized enterprises (MSMEs), which often serve as suppliers to the larger companies. This was found to be the case for Cambodia's garment industry, Indonesia's automotive manufacturing, the Philippines's electronics, and Viet Nam's agro-processing. Being better resourced and with stronger international networks, the larger companies in these industries tend to be in a more advanced stage of 4IR adoption and training than their smaller counterparts. Given that the large and small companies are often not in direct competition with each other—and indeed exhibit strong interdependencies—there is a compelling push for there to be knowledge transfer on 4IR adoption and skills development strategies from the larger companies to their MSME suppliers or subcontractors.
- **Adopt a gender-sensitive lens for certain industries.** The job displacement impacts of 4IR technologies in some industries were found to be particularly pronounced for female workers. This is the case for the garment manufacturing and tourism industries in Cambodia, the electronics sector in the Philippines, and the agro-processing industry in Viet Nam. As female workers in these sectors comprise a large share of the worker pool and tend to hold low-skilled jobs with high automatability risk (e.g., in cutting, trimming, and sewing in the garment manufacturing industry), they are likely to be disproportionately affected by 4IR. It is thus important that the training programs described in the recommendations incorporate gender-sensitive approaches (e.g., Recommendation 2 on industry-led TVET programs; Recommendation 4 on flexible skill certification programs; Recommendation 5 on formulation of new training approaches for vulnerable workers). They could consider teaching pedagogies that have been

demonstrated to be more effective for female learners (e.g., having female science, technology, engineering, and mathematics role models as trainers).[83]

- **Understand the variation in key skills by industry.** While certain skills are becoming more important across many industries as a result of 4IR, there are important differences between industries that the recommendations must take into account. For example, while "evaluation, judgment, and monitoring" is predicted to become the most important skill in six of the eight industries, in tourism the most important skill will be "written and verbal communication," and in electronics it will be "numeracy."

---

[83] Microsoft. 2018. *Closing the STEM Gap: Why STEM Classes and Careers Still Lack Girls and What We Can Do about It.*

Bibliography

Asian Development Bank (ADB). 2015. *Cambodia: Addressing the Skills Gap*. Mandaluyong: ADB.

———. 2018. *Asian Development Outlook 2018: How Technology Affects Jobs*. Mandaluyong: ADB.

———. 2018. *Social Protection Brief: Reducing Youth Not in Employment, Education or Training through JobStart Philippines*. Mandaluyong: ADB.

ADB and BAPPENAS (Ministry of National Development Planning, Indonesia). 2019. *Policies to Support the Development of Indonesia's Manufacturing Sector during 2020–2024*.

ADB and the Organisation for Economic Co-operation and Development (OECD). 2015. *Education in Indonesia: Rising to the Challenge*. Paris: OECD.

Aldaba, R. M. *Industry 4.0: Are We There Yet? I3S Inclusive Innovation Industrial Strategy*.

Allen, E. 2016. Raising Indonesian Labor Productivity. *Nikkei Asian Review*. 9 August.

Arbulu, I. et al. 2018. *Industry 4.0: Reinvigorating ASEAN Manufacturing for the Future*. McKinsey & Company.

Asia Philanthropy Circle. 2017. *Catalysing Productive Livelihood: A Guide to Education Interventions with an Accelerated Path to Scale and Impact*.

Asia Pacific MSME Trade Coalition. 2017. *Micro-Revolution: The New Stakeholders of Trade in APAC*.

Barber, M. 2007. *Instruction to Deliver: Fighting to Transform Britain's Public Services*. London: Methueun.

Behavioural Insights Team, Cabinet Office, and Nesta. 2015. *Easy, Attractive, Timely, Social: Four Simple Ways to Apply Behavioural Insights*.

Bonoli, G. 2019. Ensuring Economic Security in the Gig Economy. *Business Times*, 13 March.

Boston Consulting Group. 2015. *Industry 4.0: The Future of Productivity and Growth in Manufacturing Industries*.

Bureau for Employers' Activities and ILO (International Labour Organization). 2017. *ASEAN in Transformation: How Technology Is Changing Jobs and Enterprises.* The Philippines Country Brief. Geneva: ILO.

Center for Universal Education at Brookings. 2019. *Learning to Leapfrog: Innovative Pedagogies to Transform Education.*

Daly, E. and S. Singham. 2012. Delivery 2.0: The New Challenge for Governments. *McKinsey & Company.* 1 September.

Dang, V. L. and G. T. Yeo. 2018. Weighing the Key Factors to Improve Viet Nam's Logistics System. *Asian Journal of Shipping and Logistics* 34 (4). pp. 308–316.

Deloitte. 2015. *3D Opportunity Serves It Up: Additive Manufacturing and Food.*

Department of Budget and Management, Philippines. 2019. *TESDA Budget Nearly Doubles in 2019.* Press Release.

Department of Labor Employment, Philippines. 2019. *JobStart Philippines Program.*

Department of Science and Technology, Philippines. 2017. *Harmonized National Research and Development Agenda, 2017–2022.*

Department of Skills Development, Malaysia. *Malaysian Skill Certificate (SKM).*

Goehrke, S. 2018. Additive Manufacturing Is Driving the Future of the Automotive Industry. *Forbes.* 5 December.

Hasnan, L. 2019. Philippines's Fast-Growing Gig Economy. *ASEAN Post.* 21 February

Honeywell Case Studies. 2010. *YCH Group Selects Intermec Fixed Vehicle Computer to Improve Supply Chain Management.*

IT and Business Process Management Association of the Philippines (IBPAP). 2014. *Talent Deep Dive: An Analysis of Talent Availability for the Information Technology and Business Process Management Industry in 10 Provinces in the Philippines.*

International Labour Organization (ILO). 2015. *Rural Development and Employment Opportunities in Cambodia: How Can a National Employment Policy Contribute Toward Realization of Decent Work in Rural Areas?* Geneva: ILO.

———. 2018. *Cambodia Garment and Footwear Sector Bulletin.*

———. 2018. *Improving Practical Skills of Job Seekers through Apprenticeship.*

Indonesia Investments. 2018. Widodo Launches Road map for Industry 4.0: Making Indonesia 4.0. 6 April.

International Federation of Robotics. 2019. *Why Robot Sales in China Will Survive Slowdown in Car Production.* 4 April.

Iswara, M. A. and M. I. Gorbiano. 2019. Jokowi's Preemployment Card Program under Scrutiny. *Jakarta Post.* 12 August.

Jakarta Post. 2016. Five Plans to Upskill Indonesia's Workforce. 4 May.

———. 2019. Jokowi Issues Rule on Tax Deductions of Up to 300% of R&D Cost, 9 July.

KellyOCG. 2018. *From Workforce to Workfit*.

Ketelhut, D. J. et al. 2009. A Multi-User Virtual Environment for Building and Assessing Higher Order Inquiry Skills in Science. *British Journal of Educational Technology*. 20 December.

Kuczera, M. 2010. *Learning for Jobs—The OECD International Survey of VET Systems: First Results and Technical Report*. Paris: OECD.

Lee, J. W. 2016. *How Can Asia Close Its Emerging Skills Gap?* WEF Regional Agenda.

Lee, J. W. and D. Wie. 2013. *Technological Change, Skill Demand, and Wage Inequality in Indonesia*. Economics Working Paper 340. Mandaluyong: ADB.

Lee Kuan Yew School of Public Policy and Microsoft. 2016. *Technical and Vocational Education and Training in Indonesia: Challenges and Opportunities for the Future*.

Lewandowski, P. et al. 2019. *Technology, Skills and Globalization: Explaining International Differences in Routine and Non-Routine Work Using Survey Data*. IBS Working Paper 04/2019.

Lüthje, B. 2002. Electronics Contract Manufacturing: Global Production and the International Division of Labor in the Age of the Internet. *Industry and Innovation* 9 (3).

Masters, K. 2015. *The Impact of Industry 4.0 on the Automotive Industry*.

Mekong Strategy Partners and Raintree Development. 2018. *Cambodia's Vibrant Startup Ecosystem*.

Microsoft. 2018. *The Future Computed*.

———. 2018. *Closing the STEM Gap: Why STEM Classes and Careers Still Lack Girls and What We Can Do about It*.

Microsoft and AlphaBeta. 2019. *Preparing for AI: The Implications of Artificial Intelligence for Jobs and Skills in Asian Economies*.

Microsoft and International Data Corporation. 2018. *Digital Transformation to Contribute US$8 billion to the Philippines GDP by 2021*.

———. 2018. *Artificial Intelligence to Nearly Double the Rate of Innovation in Asia Pacific by 2021*.

Government of Cambodia, Ministry of Commerce. 2019. *Cambodia Trade Integration Strategy 2019–2023*.

Government of Cambodia, National Employment Agency. 2017. *Skills Shortages and Skills Gaps in the Cambodian Labour Market: Evidence from Employer Survey 2017*.

Government of Cambodia, National Institute of Statistics. 2015. *Cambodia Socio Economic Survey 2015*.

———. 2017. *Cambodia Socio-Economic Survey 2017*.

Government of Indonesia, Ministry of Industry. 2010. *National Medium-Term Industrial Development Plan 2015–2019*.

———. 2015. *National Industrial Development Master Plan 2015–2035*.

———. 2018. *Making Indonesia 4.0*.

Government of Indonesia, Ministry of Manpower. 2019. *Penandatanganan Kerja Sama "BLK" Komunitas Tahap I Tahun 2019 Antara Kementerian Ketenagakerjaan Dengan Lembaga Penerima Bantuan*.

Government of Indonesia, Ministry of Research and Technology and National Agency for Research and Innovation. 2019. *Policies & Programs*.

Government of Malaysia, Ministry of Higher Education, and Malaysian Qualifications Agency. 2011. *Malaysian Qualifications Framework*.

Government of the Philippines, Philippines Statistics Authority. 2018. Summary Statistics for Manufacturing Establishments. *OpenSTAT*.

Government of the Philippines, Technical Education and Skills Development Authority (TESDA). 2018. *National Technical Education and Skills Development Plan*.

Government of Singapore, Ministry of Education. 2016. *Formation of the Council for Skills, Innovation, and Productivity*. Press Release.

Government of Singapore, Ministry of Trade and Industry. 2017. *Industry Transformation Maps*. Media Factsheet.

Ng, J. S. 2018. Focus on Skills, Not Paper Qualifications, to Embrace Technological Change: Lawrence Wong. *Straits Times*. 5 May.

Organisation for Economic Co-operation and Development (OECD). 2012. *Skills Development Pathways in Asia*. Paris: OECD.

———. 2017. *Financial Incentives for Steering Education and Training, Getting Skills Right*. Paris: OECD.

———. 2018. *The Future of Social Protection: What Works for Non-Standard Workers?* Paris.

O'Malley, M. 2018. *PayPal Releases Global Freelancer Insights*. PayPal Stories.

onebillion. *Onecourse: One App that Delivers Reading, Writing and Numeracy*.

Orbeta, A. C., K. G. Gonzales, and S. F. S Cortes. 2016. *Are Higher Education Institutions Responsive to Changes in the Labor Market?* Discussion Paper 2016-08. Quezon City: Philippine Institute for Development Studies.

Oxford Economics. 2018. *Technology and the Future of ASEAN Jobs.*

Oxford Internet Institute. 2019. *Online Labour Index.*

Pathways for Prosperity Commission. 2019. *Positive Disruption: Health and Education in the Digital Age.*

Payoneer. 2019. *The Global Gig Economy Index*: Q2 2019.

Prospera and AlphaBeta. 2019. *Capturing Indonesia's Automation Potential.*

RAND. 2018. *Indonesian Family Life Survey.*

Rodrigo, P. 2017. *Half of All Indonesian Employees "May Be Underqualified."* CIPD.

Schwab, K. 2017. *The Fourth Industrial Revolution.* New York: Currency.

Sekretariat Kabinet Republik Indonesia. 2016. *Presidential Decree No. 9 Year 2016 on "Revitalizing SMKs to Improve the Quality and Competitiveness of Indonesian Human Resources."*

Skillsfuture Singapore. 2019. *Funding Support for Employers.*

SkillsFuture. 2019. Skills Framework.

Spector, J. M. and S. Ma. 2019. Inquiry and Critical Thinking Skills for the Next Generation: From Artificial Intelligence Back to Human Intelligence. *Smart Learning Environments* 6 (8).

Sullivan, R. 2019. *Increased Role of Robots in Food Manufacturing.*

Tang, S. K. 2019. Singapore Businesses Not Investing Enough in Employee Training: SBF Survey. *Channel News Asia.* 17 January.

Tran, T. 2019. Vietnam's Food Processing Industry: Promising for Foreign Investors. *SEAvestor.* 13 June.

Triyono, M. B. and Murniai, D. E. 2018. Alignment of the Curriculum to the Development of the Industrial World (Revitalization Program of Vocational High Schools in Indonesia). *TVET-Online.*

United Nations Educational, Scientific and Cultural Organization (UNESCO). 2017. *Towards Quality Assurance of Technical and Vocational Education and Training.* Paris: UNESCO.

UNESCO Institute for Lifelong Learning. 2017. *Lifelong Learning in Transformation: Promising Practices in Southeast Asia.* Paris: UNESCO.

USAID and FHI360. 2015. *Workforce Connections—Analysis of Skills Demand in Indonesia.*

World Economic Forum (WEF). 2018. *The Future of Jobs Report 2018.*

———. 2019. *Towards a Reskilling Revolution: Industry-Led Action for the Future of Work.*

WEF and A. T. Kearney. 2018. *Readiness for the Future of Production Report 2018.*

Woetzl, J. et al. 2014. *Southeast Asia at the Crossroads: Three Paths to Prosperity.* McKinsey Global Institute. November.

World Bank. 2014. *Efficient Logistics—A Key to Viet Nam's Competitiveness.* Washington, DC: World Bank.

———. 2018. *Vietnam's Future Jobs: Leveraging Mega-Trends for Greater Prosperity* Vol. 3: infographic (Vietnamese).

———. *Skills Measurement Program.*

World Travel & Tourism Council. 2020. Travel and Tourism Economic Impact 2019.

Yasih, D. W. P. and A. R. Alamsyah. 2018. Can Grab and Gojek Drivers in Indonesia Build a Solid Union? *The Conversation.* 18 April.

www.ingramcontent.com/pod-product-compliance
Lightning Source LLC
Chambersburg PA
CBHW061141230426
43663CB00028B/2999